Shankara is known as Shan........... .... meaning 'one who sets the example'. He was a child prodigy, and a genius. Aged eight he was reputed to have mastered the Vedas. At sixteen he had written his commentary on the *Brahma Sutras*, and he later wrote seminal commentaries on the *Bhagavad Gita* and the principal Upanishads. He was determined to save the Vedic teaching from onslaught by Buddhists and Jains. At the age of 32 he suddenly died having established monastic orders in the four corners of India. These orders continue to flourish, and have played a great part in the spiritual heritage of India.

Sri Ramana Maharshi (1879–1950) was born into a Brahman family. In 1896 a sense of his own death led to his Self-Realisation. He then moved to the sacred mountain, Arunachala, in Tiruvannamalai, which he never left. In 1907 he was given the name Bhagavan Sri Ramana Maharshi by the famed Poet-Saint Ganapati-Muni. He is universally acknowledged as one of the greatest spiritual figures of the twentieth century.

RAMANA, SHANKARA
and the
FORTY VERSES

*The Essential Teachings
of Advaita*

**Ramana Maharshi and Shankara
Introduction by Alan Jacobs**

Watkins Publishing
London

This edition published in the UK in 2002 by
Watkins Publishing, 20 Bloomsbury Street, London, WC1B 3QA

Cover design by Echelon Design
Cover photograph © Ramana Maharshi Foundation
Designed and typeset by Echelon Design
Printed and bound in Great Britain by NFF Production

British Library Cataloguing in Publication data available

Library of Congress Cataloging in Publication data available

ISBN 1 84293 042 7

Website: www.watkinspublishing.com

CONTENTS

INTRODUCTION

Victory to Ramana! Victory to Shankara!

These beautiful names resound like a clarion call addressed to our human hearts, imploring us to awaken from the suffering dream of life. This ancient call of the Vedic Rishis echoes through the ages, as if emanating from some primeval conch-shell, and is still available for "hearing" in our own time.

Both Great Sages knew they had truly descended from the everliving root of the Primal Sage, Dakshinamurti. Shankara's *Hymn to Dakshinamurti* and Ramana's translation exemplify this connection. The first part of this book is devoted to the inspired translation that Ramana made of some of Shankara's classics.

On 12 May 1936, Oliver Lacombe visited the Maharshi at Tiruvannamalai[1]. He asked, "Is Maharshi's teaching the same as Shankara's?" The Maharshi replied, "Maharshi's teaching is only an expression of his own experience and realisation. Others have found that it tallies with Sri Shankara's."

It is not surprising that when Sri Bhagavan discovered that the Tamil literature was deficient in correct and fine translations of some of the Acharya's works, he himself translated them into Tamil for the benefit of the Tamil-speaking population at large. The distinguished Oxford scholar and University professor, Arthur Osborne, who lived at Ramanasramam for many years, translated these jewels into English; and so the English-speaking world has similarly benefited. In the first part of this book, we preface each translation with Arthur Osborne's brief intro-duction. Ramana himself has written the introduction to the great *Vivekachudamani* or the *Crest Jewel of Discrimination*, with which this book commences.

Part Two of this book is the work of the Maharshi alone. His concise *Forty Verses on Reality* are a modern Upanishad, and unmis-takably give the Advaita teaching for contemporary mankind.

S. S. Cohen, a faithful long-standing devotee and resident of Ramanasramam during his lifetime, meticulously translated them into English. He also wrote a worthy introduction to the work which requires no further embellishments, along with a masterful commentary which makes the text abundantly clear to the Western reader.

Adi Shankara played the pivotal role in the development of philosophical thought in India. As the great consolidator of the teachings of Advaita Vedanta, he occupies a unique place in the history of world religions. His lucid commentaries on the ten principal Upanishads, the *Bhagavad Gita* and the Brahma Sutras are second to none. He was also a great *Bhakta* and composed many devotional Hymns. He founded monastic orders which survive today and still inspire many in both India and the West.

Shankara was indeed a spiritual genius of the medieval age, but it is to the wholly exemplary life and teachings of Sri Ramana Maharshi that we owe the contemporary interest in Advaita Vedanta which spreads like a forest fire in the dense woods of *samsara*, both in the East and the West. His teachings centre on Self-enquiry and Surrender to the Divine. It is indeed rare that such spiritual colossi are born on this planet: an act of Divine Grace, to point the way to liberation and Self-knowledge.

We are indeed grateful to the President of Sri Ramanas-ramam, Sri Sundaram Ramanan, for so willingly granting us permission to amalgamate all these seminal works into one volume. The scriptures in this book have truly the power to awaken the mind and turn it inwards to seek the Real Self, that which is nameless and is the common birthright of every receptive man and woman today.

Alan Jacobs
Chair, Ramana Maharshi Foundation UK
London

I

RAMANA MAHARSHI'S TRANSLATIONS FROM SHANKARA

TRANSLATIONS FROM SHANKARACHARYA

In the eighth century AD pure Vēdāntic teaching, the doctrine of advaita or non-duality, which is the very essence of Hinduism, had shrunk to a low ebb and was restored to full vigour by the great spiritual master, Sri Sankara, known also as Shankaracharya (meaning 'Shankara, the Teacher'). Ramana Maharshi, being a perfect *jnāni*, that is one who is liberated from illusion and established in absolute knowledge, accepted Sri Shankara's teaching as his own. From time to time he translated one or another of his works, either spontaneously or on the request of some devotee who did not read Sanskrit and required a Tamil version.

Arthur Osborne

VIVĒKACHŪDĀMANI

This work by Shankaracharya, together with the Drik Drishya Vivēka, *was translated into Tamil prose by Bhagavan while he was still living in Virupāksha Cave. It is a very free translation, even the order of the paragraphs being changed to some extent.*

Introduction by
Sri Bhagavan Ramana Maharshi

Every being in the world yearns to be always happy and free from the taint of sorrow, and desires to get rid of bodily ailments, etc, which are not of its true nature. Further, everyone cherishes the greatest love for himself, and this love is not possible in the absence of happiness. In deep sleep, though devoid of everything, one has the experience of being happy. Yet, due to the ignorance of the real nature of one's own being, which is happiness itself, people flounder in the vast ocean of material existence, forsaking the right path that leads to happiness, and act under the mistaken belief that the way to be happy consists in obtaining the pleasures of this and the other world.

Unfortunately, however, there is no such happiness which has not the taint of sorrow. It is precisely for the purpose of pointing out the straight path to true happiness that Lord Siva, taking on the guise of Sri Shankaracharya, wrote the commentaries on the Triple Canon (*Prasthāna Traya*) of the *Vēdānta*, which extol the excellence of this bliss; and that he demonstrated it by his own example in life. These commentaries, however, are of little use to those ardent seekers who are intent upon realizing the bliss of liberation but have not the scholarship necessary for studying them.

It is for such as these that Sri Shankara revealed the essence of the commentaries in this short treatise, *The Crown Gem of Discrimination*, explaining in detail the points that have to be grasped by those who seek liberation, and thereby directing them to the true and direct path.

Sri Shankara begins by observing that it is hard indeed to attain human birth, and that, having attained it, one should strive to achieve the bliss of liberation, which is really only the nature of one's being. By *jnāna* or spiritual knowledge alone, is this Bliss to be realized, and *jnāna* is achieved only through *vichāra* or steady enquiry. In order to learn this method of enquiry, says Sri Shankara, one should seek the grace of a guru; and he then proceeds to describe the qualities of the guru and his disciple and how the latter should approach and serve his master. He further emphasizes that in order to realize the bliss of liberation one's own individual effort is an essential factor. Mere book-learning never yields this bliss; it can be realized only through Self-enquiry or *vichāra*, which consists of *sravana* or devoted attention to the percepts of the guru, *manana* or deep contemplation and *nididhyāsana* or cultivation of equanimity in the Self.

The three bodies, are non-self and are unreal. The Self, that is the *aham* or 'I' is quite different from them. It is due to ignorance that the sense of Self or the 'I' notion is foisted on that which is not Self, and this indeed is bondage. Since from ignorance arises bondage, from knowledge ensues liberation. To know this from the guru is *sravana*.

The process of *manana*, which is subtle enquiry or deep contemplation, consists in rejecting the three bodies consisting of the five sheaths (physical, vital, mental, intellectual, and blissful), as not 'I' and discovering through subtle enquiry of 'Who am I?' that which is different from all three and exists single and universal in the heart as *aham* or 'I', just as a stalk of grass is delicately drawn out from its sheath. This 'I' is denoted by the word *tvam* (in the scriptural dictum, *Tat-tvam-asi*, 'That thou art').

The world of name and form is but an adjunct of *tat* or *Brahman* and, having no separate reality, is rejected as unreality and affirmed as nothing else by *Brahman*. The instruction of the disciple by the Guru in the Mahavakya *Tat-tvam-asi*, which declares the identity of the Self and the Supreme, is this *upadesa* (spiritual guidance). The disciple is then enjoined to remain in the beatific state *aham-Brahman*, (I – the Absolute). Nevertheless, the old tendencies of the mind sprout up thick and strong and constitute an obstruction. These tendencies are threefold and ego is their root. The ego flourishes in the externalized and differentiating consciousness caused by the forces of projection due to *rajas* and veiling due to *tamas*.

To fix the mind firmly in the heart until these forces are destroyed and to awaken with unswerving, ceaseless vigilance the true and cognate tendency which is characteristic of the *ātman* and is expressed by saying: *Aham Brahmāsmi* (I am *Brahman*), and *Brahmaivāham* (*Brahman* alone am I) is termed *nididhyāsana* or *ātmanusandhāna*, that is constancy in the Self. This is otherwise called *bhakti*, yoga and *dhyāna*.

Ātmanusandhāna has been compared to churning curds in order to make butter, the mind being compared to the churn, the heart to the curds, and the practice of concentration on the Self to the process of churning. Just as butter is made by churning the curds and fire by friction, so the natural and changeless state of *nirvikalpa samādhi* is produced by unswerving vigilant concentration on the Self, ceaseless, like the unbroken flow of oil. This readily and spontaneously yields that direct, immediate, unobstructed, and universal perception of *Brahman*, which is at once knowledge and experience and which transcends time and space.

This perception is Self-realization. Achieving it cuts the knot of the heart. The false delusions of ignorance, the vicious and age-long tendencies of the mind which constitute this knot are destroyed. All doubts are dispelled and the bondage of *karma* is severed.

Thus in this *Crown Gem of Discrimination* Sri Shankara has described *samādhi* or spiritual trance which is the limitless bliss of liberation, beyond doubt and duality, and at the same time has indicated the means for its attainment. To attain this state of freedom from duality is the real purpose of life, and only he who has done so is a *jīvanmukta*, liberated while yet alive, not one who has a mere theoretical understanding of what constitutes *purushārtha* or the desired end and aim of human endeavour.

Thus defining a *jīvanmukta*, Sri Shankara declares him to be free from the bonds of threefold karma (*sanchita, āgāmi* and *prārabdha*). The disciple attains this state and then relates his personal experience. He who is liberated is indeed free to act as he pleases, and when he leaves the body, he abides in liberation and never returns to this birth, which is death.

Sri Shankara thus describes realization, that is liberation, as twofold, *jīvanmukti* and *vidēhamukti*, as explained above. Moreover, in this short treatise, written in the form of a dialogue between a guru and his disciple, he has considered many other relevant topics.

(By courtesy of the *Sunday Times*, Madras.)

CREST JEWEL OF DISCRIMINATION

Invocation

Rejoice eternally!! The heart rejoices at the feet of the Lord, who is the Self, shining within as 'I-I' eternally, so that there is no alternation of night and day. This will result in removal of ignorance of the Self.

Praise to the Guru

Sri Shankara Jagathguru shines as the form of Lord Siva. In this work, *Vivēkachudāmani*, he has expounded in detail the heart of *Vēdānta* and its meaning in order that the most ardent of those qualified for liberation may acquaint themselves with it and attain immortality.

Homage to the ever blissful Sri Govinda Sadguru who is to be known only by the ultimate truth of *Vēdānta* and not by any other standard.

The Text

It is indeed very difficult to obtain a human body. Even though one does, it is very difficult to become a Brahmin. Even if one becomes one, it is still more difficult to walk in the path of *vaidik dharma* in which the Vedas are chanted. Still more difficult is it to become a perfect scholar, and more difficult again to undertake enquiry into the Self and the non-Self. Yet more difficult than all this is to obtain wisdom born of experience of the Self. Liberation in the form of abidance as the Self, born of that wisdom, is not to be attained except as a result of righteous actions performed throughout countless crores of births. However, even though all the above qualifications may not be obtained, liberation is assured through the grace of the Lord if only three conditions are obtained: that is a human birth, intense desire for liberation, and association with sages.

If, by some great penance, that rarity, a human body is obtained, with its ability to understand the meaning of the scriptures, and yet, owing to attachment to insentient things, effort is not made to attain the immutable state of liberation, which is one's own true state, then indeed one is a fool committing suicide. What greater fool is there than one who does not seek his own good?

Liberation is not to be achieved through endless cycles of time by reading the scriptures or worshipping the gods or by anything else than knowledge of the unity of *Brahman* and *ātman*. Wealth or actions made possible by wealth cannot produce the yearning for liberation. Therefore the scriptures have rightly declared that action can never produce liberation. In order to obtain liberation one must heroically renounce even the very desire for the pleasures of this world. Then one must seek the perfect guru who is the embodiment of peace and must concentrate one's mind and meditate ceaselessly on that into which one is initiated. Such meditation leads to abidance in the wisdom of the experience obtained. Embarking in that ship of wisdom, one must ferry over to the shore of liberation that Self which is immersed in the ocean of *samsāra*. Therefore the courageous aspirant should give up attachment to wife, sons and property and give up all activity. By so doing he should free himself from bondage to the cycle of birth and death and seek liberation. Actions are prescribed only for purification of the mind, not for realization of the Self. Knowledge of the truth of the Self is obtained only by Self-enquiry and not by any number of actions. One who mistakes a rope for a serpent is cast into fear thereby and his fear and distress can be removed only by the knowledge that it is a rope. A friend who knows this tells him so and he investigates and finds that it is so. There is no other way. Similarly, knowledge of Brahman is obtained through initiation by the Guru and enquiry into Truth. That Truth cannot be realized through purificatory baths, offerings, breath-control, or any other practice. He who seeks liberation through knowledge of the Self must enquire into the Self with the help of the perfect Guru who, being free from desires, is a knower of *Brahman* and an ocean of grace. It is mainly through enquiry that he who is competent achieves knowledge of the Self; circumstance, time, and the grace of the Lord are but aids to the quest.

In order to be qualified for enquiry into the Self, a man must have a powerful intellect and ability to seize the essential and reject the inessential besides the various qualities enumerated in the scriptures. What are these? He must be able to discriminate between the real and the unreal. He must have an unattached mind. He must ardently desire liberation. And he must be tireless in practice. Only such a one is qualified to enquire into *Brahman*. The qualifications are enumerated as follows:

1. Discrimination between the real and the unreal.
2. Disinclination to enjoy the fruits of one's actions either in this or in any further life.
3. The six virtues of tranquillity, self-control, withdrawal, forbearance, faith, and concentration of the Self.
4. Intense yearning for liberation.

The aspirant must indeed have these qualities in order to attain abidance in the Self; without them there can be no realization of the Truth. Let us see what these are:

1. Discrimination between the real and the unreal is the firm conviction that *Brahman* alone is the Truth and that the world is unreal.
2. We both observe and learn from the scriptures that all pleasures experienced by animate beings, from Brahma downwards, are transient and impermanent and involve sorrows and imperfections; giving up the desire for them is *vairāgya* or non-attachment.
3. (a) Tranquillity implies fixing the mind upon its target by meditating frequently on the imperfections of things and becoming dissatisfied with them.

    (b) Self-control means controlling the outer and inner sense organs and fixing them in their respective centres.

    (c) Withdrawal means giving up all outer activity by fixing the mind on its target so firmly that it is not led by its previous tendencies to dwell on objects.

    (d) Forbearance means the endurance of any sorrows that may befall without trying to avoid them.

    (e) Faith, which is the cause of Self-realization, is the outcome of firm conviction of the truth of *Vēdāntic* scriptures and of the words of the Guru.

    (f) Concentration is making every effort to fix the mind on the pure *Brahman* despite its wandering nature.

These are said to be the six qualifications needed for the practice of *samādhi*.

4. Intense yearning for liberation arises from the desire to free oneself by realizing one's true nature, attaining freedom from the bondage of the body and ego which is caused by ignor-

ance. This yearning may be of different grades. It may be only dull or medium, but it may be highly developed by means of the six qualifications mentioned above, and in this case it can bear fruit. But if renunciation and yearning are weak, the result may be mere appearance like a mirage in the desert.

Of all the means leading to liberation, *bhakti* or devotion is the best; and this *bhakti* means seeking the truth of one's own Self, so say the sages.

The aspirant who possesses the necessary qualifications and wishes to undertake Self-enquiry must seek a Sadguru and bow down to him with humility, awe, and reverence and serve him in various ways. The Sadguru is one capable of destroying the bondage of those who adhere to him. He is an ocean of immutable wisdom. His knowledge is all-comprehensive. He is pure as crystal.

He has attained victory over desires. He is supreme among the knowers of *Brahman*. He rests calmly in *Brahman* like a fire that has consumed its fuel. He is an endless reservoir of mercy. There is no explanation why he is merciful; it is his very nature. He befriends all sadhus who adhere to him. To such a Guru the disciple appeals: 'I bow down to you, my Master, true friend of the helpless! I pray you to help me cross the terrible ocean of bondage into which I have fallen and by which I am overwhelmed. A mere gracious look from you is a raft that will save me. Oh flowing stream of Grace! I am shaken violently by the winds of a perverse fate. I do not know which way to turn. I am tormented by the unquenchable fire of *samsāra* that burns around me. I continually pray to you to calm me by the nectar of your grace. Sadhus such as you who abide ever in peace, are great and magnanimous and constantly benefit the world, like the season of spring. Not only have they themselves crossed the ocean of *samsāra*, but they can calm the fears of others. Just as the world after being heated by the burning rays of the sun is calmed by the cool and gracious rays of the moon, so also it is in your nature to give protection for no reason whatever to people like me who have taken refuge with you from the ocean of *samsāra*. Indeed, being helpless and having no other refuge, I have cast on you the burden of protecting me from this *samsāra* of birth and death. Oh Lord! the flames of the conflagration of individual being have scorched me; cool me through the outpouring of your gracious words. Your words bring peace, being born of your experience of divine bliss. Blessed are they that have even received your gracious glance. Blessed are they who have become acceptable to you. How shall I cross the ocean and what means is there? I do not indeed know what is my fate. You alone must protect me, setting me free from this sorrow of *samsāra*.'

The disciple thus takes refuge with the Guru, as enjoined by the scriptures. He waits upon the Guru, unable to bear the burning winds of *samsāra*. His mind grows calm through following the Guru's bidding. The teacher, that is, the knower of Brahman, casts upon him his gracious glance and touches his soul inwardly, giving him assurance of protection. 'My learned disciple, have no fear. No harm shall come to you hereafter. I will give you a single mighty means by which you can cross this terrible, fathomless ocean of *samsāra* and thus obtain supreme Bliss. By this means, world-renouncing sadhus have crossed it and your bondage also shall be destroyed here and now. The scriptures declare: "The means of liberation for seekers are faith, devotion, meditation, and yoga." You too shall obtain these means, and if you practise them constantly shall be set free from the bondage to the body caused by ignorance. You are eternally of the nature of Paramātma and this bondage of *samsāra*, of non-Self, has come upon you only through ignorance. It will be utterly destroyed by knowledge born of enquiry into the Self.'

Gazing on the Guru who says this, the disciple asks: 'Oh

Master, what is bondage? How did it come, how does it survive, and how is it to be destroyed? What is the non-Self? And what, indeed, is the Self? And what is discrimination between Self and non-Self? Graciously bless me with answers to these questions, so that by hearing your replies I may be blessed.'

To this request of the disciple the Master answers: 'Dear soul! If you have felt the desire to be the Self, free from the bondage caused by ignorance, you are indeed blessed. You have achieved life's purpose. You have sanctified thereby your whole line. Just as sons and other relations pay off the debts of a father, so there are others who will free one from bearing a burden on one's head. But the distress caused by hunger can be cured only by eating for oneself, not by others eating for one. And if you are sick you must take medicine and keep a proper diet yourself; no one else can do it for you. Similarly, bondage comes to you through your own ignorance and can only be removed by yourself. However learned a man may be, he cannot rid himself of the ignorance born of desire and fate, except by realizing *Brahman* with his own infinite knowledge. How does it help you if others see the moon? You must open your eyes and see it for yourself. Liberation cannot be obtained through *sankhya*, yoga, ritual, or learning but only through knowledge of the oneness of Brahman and *ātman*. Just as the beautiful form of the *veena* and the music of its strings only give pleasure to people, but confer no kingdom on them, so also plausible words, clever arguments, ability to expound the scriptures, and the erudition of the learned only give pleasure for the moment. Even study of the scriptures is useless since it does not give the desired result. Once one knows the truth of the Supreme, study of the scriptures becomes unnecessary because there is nothing more to be gained. Therefore one must pass over the great forest of the *sāstras*, which only yields confusion of mind, and must instead actually experience the Self through the Guru, who is a knower of reality. To one who is bitten by the serpent of ignorance, salvation can come only from the elixir of Self-knowledge and not from the Vedas, scriptures, incantations, or any other remedies. Just as a person's sickness is not removed without taking medicine, so too his state of bondage is not removed by scriptural texts such as "I am *Brahman*" without his own direct experience of the Self. One does not become a king by merely saying: "I am a king", without destroying one's enemies and obtaining the reality of power. Similarly, one does not obtain liberation as *Brahman* itself by merely repeating the scriptural text "I am *Brahman*", without destroying the duality caused by ignorance and directly experiencing the Self. A treasure trove hidden under the ground is not obtained by merely hearing about it, but only by being told by a friend who knows it, and then digging and removing the slab that hides it and taking it out from below the ground. Similarly, one must hear about one's true state from a Guru who knows *Brahman*, and then meditate upon it and experience it directly through constant meditation. Without this, the true form of one's own Self, that is hidden by *māyā*, cannot be realized through mere argumentation. Therefore, those who are wise themselves make every effort to remove the bondage of individual existence and obtain liberation, just as they would get rid of some disease.

'Beloved disciple, the question that you have put is of the utmost importance and acceptable to realized souls well versed in the scriptures. It is like an aphorism bearing a subtle meaning and understandable to him who craves liberation. Listen to this reply with a calm and undisturbed mind and your bonds will be cut asunder at once. The primary means of obtaining liberation is *vairāgya* (dispassion). Other qualities such as tranquillity, self-control, forbearance, and renunciation of activity can come later, later again the hearing of *Vēdāntic* truth, and still later, meditation on that truth. Finally comes perpetual and prolonged meditation on *Brahman*. This gives rise to *nirvikalpa samādhi*, through which is

attained the strength for direct realization of the supreme Self.
This power of direct realization enables the discriminating soul
to experience the bliss of liberation here and now. Such is the
sādhana leading to liberation.

'Now I shall tell you about discrimination between Self and
non-Self. Listen and keep it firmly in mind. Of these two I shall
speak first about the non-Self.

'The brain, bones, fat, flesh, blood, skin, and semen are the
seven factors that constitute the gross body. So say those who
know. The feet, thighs, chest, shoulders, back, head, etc, are its
members. People regard it as "I" owing to the mind's attachment
to it. It is the primary attraction to all, and the most obvious.
It is made up of ether, air, fire, water, and earth which, as the
subtle essences, form sense objects, and the groups of five such
as sound, touch, sight, taste, and smell. The ego (*jiva*) being
intent on pleasure, regards these as means of enjoyment. Foolish
and ignorant persons are bound to sense objects by the rope of
desire, attracted according to the power of their *karma* which
leads them up and down and causes them to wander in distress.
The serpent and deer die through attachment to sound, the
elephant through attachment to touch, the fish through attachment to taste, and the bee through attachment to smell. If these
die through attachment to a single sense, what must be the fate
of man, who is attached to all five? The evil effects of sense
objects are more harmful than the poison of the cobra,[1] because
poison only kills him who takes it, whereas sense objects bring
destruction to him who only sees them or even thinks of them.
He alone obtains liberation who, with the sharp sword of detachment, cuts the strong rope of love for sense objects and so frees
himself from them. Otherwise, even though a man be well versed
in all the six *sāstras*, he will not obtain liberation. Desire, like a
crocodile, instantly seizes the aspirant after liberation who tries
to cross the ocean of *samsāra* and reach the shore of liberation

without firm detachment, and straightaway drags him down into the ocean. Only that aspirant who kills the crocodile with the keen sword of detachment can cross the ocean and safely reach the shore of liberation. He who, lacking good sense, enters upon one path after another of attachment to sense objects, experiences ever greater distress until he is finally destroyed. But he who exerts control over himself, walks on the path of discrimination laid down by the Guru and attains his goal. This indeed is the truth. Therefore, if you really want liberation cast away the pleasure of sense objects as though they were poison. Hold firmly to the virtues of contentment, compassion, forgiveness, sincerity, tranquillity, and self-control. Give up all actions performed out of attachment to the body, and strive ceaselessly for liberation from the bondage caused by ignorance. This body is finally consumed, whether by earth, fire, beasts, or birds. He who, forgetting his real nature, mistakes this body for the Self, gets attached to it and cherishes it and by so doing becomes the murderer of the Self. He who still cares for the body while seeking the Self, is like one who catches hold of a crocodile to cross a river. Infatuation with the body is indeed fatal to the aspirant after liberation. Only he who overcomes this infatuation attains liberation. Therefore, you too must overcome infatuation for the body and for wife and children. Then you will attain liberation, i.e. the supreme state of Vishnu which the great sages have attained. This gross body is very much to be deprecated, consisting as it does of skin, flesh, blood, arteries and veins, fat, marrow and bones, and is full of urine and excreta. It is produced by one's own past actions out of the gross elements. The subtle elements unite together to produce these gross elements. Thus it becomes a habitation for the enjoyment of pleasures by the ego, like his home for a householder. It is in the waking state that the ego experiences the gross body. It is in this state alone that it can be experienced, when the Self, though really separate from it, is

deluded into identifying itself with it and, through the external
organs, enjoys the various wonderful gross objects of pleasure
such as garlands, sandal-paste, woman, etc. Know that the whole
of outward *samsara* comes upon the spirit (*purusha*) through the
medium of the gross body. Birth, growth, old age, decay, and
death are its characteristics. Childhood, boyhood, youth, and old
age are its stages. Castes and orders of life are ordained for it. It
is also subject to different modes of treatment, to honour and
dishonour, and is the abode of various diseases.

'The ears, skin, eyes, nose, and tongue are organs of knowledge
because they enable us to cognize objects. The vocal organs,
hands, feet, etc, are organs of action because they perform their
respective modes of action. The internal organ (mind) is single in
itself but is variously named mind, intellect, ego, or desire (*chitta*).
Mind is the faculty of desire or repulsion. Intellect is the faculty
of determining the truth of things. The ego is the faculty which
identifies itself with the body as self. Desire (*chitta*) is the faculty
that seeks for pleasure. Just as gold and silver are shaped into
various forms, so the single life-breath becomes *prāna, apāna,
vyāna, udāna, samāna*. The group of five elements (ether, fire,
water, air, earth), the group of five organs of knowledge (ears,
eyes, skin, nose, tongue), the group of five organs of action
(vocal organs, hands, feet, anus, genitals), the group of five vital
airs (*prāna, apāna, vyāna, udāna, samāna*), the group of four
internal organs (*chittā, manas, buddhi, ahankāra*), all these together
compose the subtle body called the city of eight constituents.
Being possessed of desires, it is produced out of the elements
prior to their sub-division and mutual combin-ation. The soul
has brought this beginningless superimposition upon itself by
its actions. This state of experience is the dream state. In this
state the mind functions of its own accord, experiencing itself as
the actor, due to its various tendencies and to the effect of
experiences of the waking state. In this state the Self, shining

with its own light, is superimposed upon the mind without being attached to its actions and remains a mere witness. Just as the axe and other tools of the carpenter are only the means for his activities, so this subtle body is only the means for the activities of the Self which is ever aware. The internal organs perform all their actions owing to the mere proximity of the Self, whereas the Self remains unaffected and untouched by these actions. Good or bad eyesight is due to the state of the eyes, deafness to the ears, and so on; they do not affect the Self, the knower. Those who know say that inhalation, exhalation, yawning, sneezing, etc, are functions of the life-breath, as also are hunger and thirst. The inner organ (mind), with the light of reflected consciousness, has its seat in the outer organs, such as the eye, and identifies itself with them. This inner organ is the ego. The ego is the actor and enjoyer, identifying itself with the body as "I". Under the influence of the three *gunas* it assumes the three states of waking, dream and deep sleep. When sense objects are to its liking it becomes happy, when not, unhappy. Thus, pleasure and pain pertain to the ego and are not characteristics of the ever-blissful Self. Objects appear to be pleasant because of the Self and not because of any inherent bliss that is in them. The Self has no grief in it. Its bliss, which is independent of objects, is experienced by everyone in the state of deep sleep and therefore it is dear to everyone. This is borne out by the authority of the Upanishads and by direct perception, tradition, and inference.

'The Supreme (*Brahman*) has a wonderful *shakti* (power or energy) known as "the undifferentiated", "ignorance", "*māyā*", etc. She is of the form of the three *gunas*. Her existence is inferred by those of understanding from the effects produced by her. She is far superior to all objectivity and creates the entire universe. She is neither being nor non-being, neither does she partake of the nature of both. She is neither composed of parts nor indivisible nor both. She is neither form nor formless nor both. She is none of these.

Such as she is, she is indescribable. She is also beginningless. Yet just as the deluded fear of a snake in a piece of rope is removed by recognizing the rope as such, so too *māyā* may be destroyed by integral knowledge of *Brahman*. She has her three *gunas* which are to be known from their effects. *Rajas*, whose colour is red, is of the nature of activity and is the power of projection. It is the original cause of all activity. From it arise the mental modifications that lead to desires and sorrows. Lust, anger, grasping, pride, hatred, egotism are all tendencies characteristic of *rajas*. This projecting power is the cause of bondage because it creates outward or worldly tendencies. *Tamas*, whose colour is black, is the veiling power. It makes things appear other than what they are. Through its alliance with the power of projection, it is the original cause of man's constant rebirth. He who is enveloped by this veiling power, wise or learned though he may be, clever, expert in the meaning of the scriptures, capable of wonderful achievements, will not be able to grasp the truth of the Self, even though the Guru and others clearly explain it in various ways. Being under the sway of that veiling power, he esteems things which bear the imprint of delusion and ignorance and achieves them. Even though he is taught, he who is enveloped by this veiling power still lacks the clear knowledge and understanding without which it cannot be removed; he always remains in doubt and comes to decisions contrary to the truth. At the same time, the power of projection makes him restless. Ignorance, indolence, inertia, sleepiness, omission of the discharge of duties, and stupidity are the characteristics of *tamas*. One who has these qualities does not comprehend anything but is like a sleeping man or a stone. Now, coming to *sattva*, whose colour is *white*: although this is quite clear like pure water, yet it gets murky if mixed with *rajas* and *tamas*. The Self shines through *sattva* just as the sun illumines the entire world of matter. Even from mixed *sattva* virtuous qualities result, such as modesty, *yama* and *niyama*, faith, devotion and the desire for devotion, divine qualities and turning away from the unreal. From the clarity of pure *sattva* results Self-realization, supreme peace, never failing contentment, perfect happiness, abiding in the Self which is the fount of eternal bliss. The undifferentiated power which is spoken of as a compound of the three *gunas* is the causal body of the soul. Its state is that of deep sleep in which all the sense organs and functions of the mind are at rest. In this state all perceptions cease and the mind in its subtle seed-like form experiences supreme bliss. This is borne out by the universal experience, "I slept soundly and knew nothing."

'The above is a description of the non-Self. These things do not pertain to the Self: the body, the sense organs, the mind, the ego and its modes, happiness due to sense objects, the elements from ether downwards, and the whole world up to the undifferentiated *māyā*. All this is non-Self. From *mahat* (cosmic intelligence) down to the gross body, everything is the effect of *māyā*. Know these to be the non-Self. These are all unreal like a mirage in the desert.

'Now I am going to tell you about the real nature of the supreme Self, by realizing which, man attains liberation and is freed from bondage. That realization of "I" is indeed the Self which is experienced as "I-I" shining of its own accord, the absolute Being, the witness of the three states of waking, dream, and deep sleep, distinct from the five sheaths, aware of the mental modes in the waking and dream states, and of their absence in the state of deep sleep. That Self sees all of its own accord but is never seen by any of these. It gives light to the intellect and ego but is not enlightened by them. It pervades the universe and by its light all this insentient universe is illumined, but the universe does not pervade it even to the slight extent. In its presence the body, senses, mind, and intellect enter upon their functions as if commanded by it. By that unbroken knowledge, all things from the ego to the body, objects and our experience of

them, occur and are perceived. By it life and the various organs
are set in motion. That inner Self, as the primeval spirit, external,
ever effulgent, full and infinite Bliss, single, indivisible, whole
and living, shines in everyone as the witnessing awareness. That
Self in its splendour, shining in the cavity of the heart as the
subtle, pervasive yet unmanifest ether, illumines this universe
like the sun. It is aware of the modifications of the mind and ego,
of the actions of the body, sense organs and life-breath. It takes
their form as fire does that of a heated ball of iron; yet it
undergoes no change in doing so. This Self is neither born nor
dies, it neither grows nor decays, nor does it suffer any change.
When a pot is broken the space inside it is not, and similarly,
when the body dies, the Self in it remains eternal. It is distinct
from the causal *māyā* and its effects. It is pure knowledge. It
illumines Being and non-being alike and is without attributes. It
is the witness of the intellect in the waking, dream, and deep
sleep states. It shines as "I-I", as ever-present, direct experience.
Know that supreme Self by means of a one-pointed mind and
know "This 'I' is *Brahman*". Thus through the intellect you may
know the Self in yourself, by yourself, and by this means cross
the ocean of birth and death and become one who has achieved
his life purpose and ever remain as the Self.

'Mistaking the body or not-I for the Self or I, is the cause of
all misery, that is, of all bondage. This bondage comes through
ignorance of the cause of birth and death, for it is through
ignorance that men regard these insentient bodies as real,
mistaking them for the Self and sustaining them with sense
objects and finally getting destroyed by them, just as the silk-
worm protects itself by the threads that it emits, but is finally
destroyed by them. For those who mistake the rope for a serpent,
the integral pure effulgence of the pristine state is veiled by *tamas*,
just as the dragon's head covers the sun in an eclipse, and as a
result, the spirit (*purusha*) forgets his reality. He is devoured by

the dragon of delusion and, mistaking the non-self for the Self, is overpowered by mental states and submerged in the fathomless ocean of *samsāra* full of the poison of sense-enjoyments, and, now sinking, now rising, he finds no way of escape. Such are the torments caused by the projecting power of *rajas* together with the veiling of *tamas*. Just as the layers of clouds caused by the rays of the sun increase until they hide the sun itself, so the bondage of ego caused by ignorance in the Self expands until it hides that very Self. Just as frost and cold winds torment one on a wintry day when the sun is hidden by clouds, so too when *tamas* covers the Self, the projecting power of *rajas* deludes the ignorant into mistaking the non-Self for the Self and torments them with many sorrows. So it is by these two powers alone that the Self has been brought into bondage. Of this tree of *samsāra*, *tamas* is the seed, the "I am the body" idea is the shoot, desire is the young leaf, activity the water that makes it grow, the body the trunk, a man's successive lives the branches, the sense organs the twigs, sense objects the flowers, and diverse sorrows caused by activity the fruit. The ego is the bird sitting in the tree and enjoying its fruit.

'This bondage of the non-Self, born of ignorance, causing endless sorrow through birth, death, and old age, is without beginning, yet its complete destruction can be brought about in the way that I will tell you. Have faith in the Vedas and perform all the actions prescribed by them without seeking for any gain from doing so. This will give you purity of mind. With this pure mind, meditate incessantly and by doing so you will directly know the Self. This Self-knowledge is the keen sword that cuts asunder the bonds. No other weapon or contrivance is capable of destroying them, nor wind nor fire nor countless actions.

'The Self is covered over by the five sheaths caused by the power of ignorance. It is hidden from sight like the water of a pond covered with weeds. When the weeds are removed the water is revealed and can be used by man to quench his thirst and cool him from the heat. In the same way, by process of elimination, you should with keen intellect discard the objective five sheaths from the Self as "not this, not this". Know the Self distinct from the body and from all forms, like a stalk of grass in its sheaths of leaf. Know it as eternal, pure, single in its essence, unattached, with no duties to perform, ever blissful and self-effulgent. He who is liberated realizes that all objective reality, which is super-imposed on the Self as the idea of a serpent is on the rope, is really no other than the Self, and he himself is the Self. Therefore the wise aspirant should undertake discrimination between the Self and the non-Self. Of the five sheaths (food, life-breath, mind, intellect, and bliss), the gross body is created out of food, increasing by eating it and perishing when there is none. It is the sheath of food. Compounded of skin, blood, flesh, fat, marrow, excreta, and urine, it is most filthy. It has no existence before birth or after death but appears between them. It undergoes change every moment. There is no set law governing that change. It is an object, like a pot, is insentient and has a variety of forms. It is acted upon by other forces. The Self, on the other hand, is distinct from this body and is single, eternal, and pure. It is indestructible, though the body with its limbs is destroyed. The Self is the witness who knows the characteristics of the body, its modes of activity and its three states. It is self-aware and directs the body. Such being the contrast between the body and the Self, how can the body be the Self? The fool thinks of it as the Self. The man of wise action with some measure of discrimination, takes body and soul together for "I", but the really wise man who conducts the enquiry with firm discrimination knows himself always as the supreme *Brahman*, the Being which is of its own nature. The "I am the body" idea is the seed of all sorrow. Therefore, just as you do not identify yourself with your shadow body, image body, dream body, or the body that you have in your imagination, cease also to associate the Self in any way with the body of skin, flesh, and bones. Make every effort to root out this error and holding fast to the knowledge of reality as the absolute *Brahman*, destroy the mind and obtain supreme peace. Then you will have no more births. Even a learned scholar who perfectly understands the meaning of *Vēdānta* has no hope of liberation if, owing to delusion, he cannot give up the idea of the non-existent body as the Self.

'Now we come to the vital body of *prāna*, which is the life-breath with the five organs of action. The aforementioned sheath of food enters upon its course of activity when filled by this vital force. It is nothing but a modification of air, and like air it enters into the body and comes out of it. It does not know its own desires and antipathies or those of others. It is eternally dependent on the Self. Therefore the vital body cannot be the Self.

'The mental sheath is the mind with its organs of knowledge. This is the cause of the wrong concept of the Self as "I" and "mine". It is very powerful, being endowed with diversity of thought-forms, beginning with the I-thought. It fills and pervades the vital sheath. The ever-blazing fire of the mental sheath is consuming this whole world, lit by the five sense organs as sacrificial priests, fed by sense objects as the fuel, and kept ablaze by the latent tendencies. There is no ignorance apart from the mind. It is the cause of the bondage of birth and death. With the emergence of the mind everything arises, and with its subsidence everything ceases. In the dream state, in which there are no objects, the mind creates its dream world of enjoyers and others, by its own powers. Similarly, all that it perceives in the waking state is its own display. It is the experience of all that nothing appears when the mind subsides in deep sleep. Therefore the bondage of *samsāra* is only superimposed on the Self by the mind. Actually it has no reality. Just as the wind gathers the clouds in the sky and then disperses them, so the mind causes the bondage but also causes liberation. The mind first creates in man an attachment to the body and to all sense objects, with the result that he is bound by his attachment like a beast tethered by a rope. Under the influence of *rajas* and *tamas* it is enfeebled and entangles man in desire for the body and objects, but under the influence of *sattva* it breaks away from *rajas* and *tamas* and attains to non-attachment and discrimination and rejects sense objects as though they were poison. Therefore the wise seeker after liberation must first establish himself in discrimination and desirelessness. The mind is a great tiger roaming wild in the huge jungle of sense objects. Therefore aspirants should keep away from it. It is only the mind that conjures up before the Self subtle and gross objects and all the variations of body, caste, and station in life, qualities and action, causes and effects. So doing, it tempts and deludes the Self, which is really unattached pure intelligence, binding it by the qualities of body, senses, and life and deluding it with the idea of "I" and "mine" in the fruits of action that it creates. By means of this false representation, the mind creates the myth of *samsāra* (bondage) for the spirit. This is the primal cause of the sorrow of birth and death which binds those who are subject to the faults of *rajas* and *tamas* and lack discrimination. Just as cloud masses revolve through the air, so does the whole world revolve through the delusion of the mind. Therefore, those who know reality declare that the mind is ignorance. He who seeks liberation must examine his mind by his own efforts and once the mind is purified by such introspection liberation is obtained and appears obvious and natural. Out of desire for liberation you should root out all other desires, renounce activity and take to perpetual preoccupation with Truth (*sravana manana*) which will lead on to perpetual meditation (*nididhyāsana*). Then alone can the waves of the mind be stilled. Therefore even this mind sheath cannot be the real Self, since it has a beginning and an end, and is subject to modifications and characterized by pain and grief, and is an object of perception.

'The intellect with the five organs of knowledge is the *vijnāna māyā* sheath and is also the cause of bondage for the spirit. It is a modification of the unmanifest, beginningless Self which has assumed the form of the ego and conducts all activities through the reflected light of consciousness. It is the conscious agent of activity and its attributes are intelligence and actions. It regards the body and senses as "I" and their mode of life, duties, actions, and qualities as "mine". It performs good or evil actions as dictated by its previous tendencies, and as a result of these actions attains to higher or lower regions and wanders there until it is attracted to re-birth in some enticing womb. It experiences the states of waking, dream, and deep sleep and the pleasant and painful fruits of its actions. Within this sheath of knowledge, the Self throbs as the self-effulgent light, the supreme soul, homogeneous, the Truth, all pervasive, complete, immutable, the supreme Lord. Yet the Self assumes limitations through the false superimposition of the intellect on it in this sheath, because this is close to it, and in fact the closest of its adjuncts. As a result it is deluded into thinking that it is this sheath. Just as a pot might seem to be different from its clay, so it imagines itself to be different from itself, to be the agent and the enjoyer, and seems to be limited in such ways, although it is like the fire in a ball of hot iron, unaffected by the shape of the ball."

In answer to the Guru, the disciple says: 'Master, I accept your statement that, whether through delusion or not, the supreme Self has come to regard itself as the ego. But since this super-imposition of the ego-concept is beginningless, it cannot be supposed to have an end either. How, then, can there be liberation? But if there is no liberation the ego-concept becomes eternal and bondage also becomes eternal. Pray enlighten me on this point.'

To this the Master replies: 'That is a good question, my learned disciple. Now listen with one-pointed mind to my explanation. Whatever has been conjured up by delusion must be examined in the pure light of reason. Things appear real as long as the delusion lasts and perish as unreal and non-existent as soon as it passes, just like illusion of a serpent seen in a piece of rope and appearing real as long as the illusion lasts. Really the Self is unattached, actionless, characterless, immutable, formless, Being-Consciousness-Bliss, the inner witness. It has no sort of relationship with anything. To think that it has is a mere delusion like the appearance of blue in the sky. The false attitude of the ego to the Self is due to the relationship with the beginningless false vehicle, but even this sense of relationship is the result of delusion. Although this attitude of the ego to the Self is without a beginning, that does not make it real. Just as water becomes clear as soon as the dirt is removed from it, so is it with the Self when the effects of the ego and its false adjuncts are dropped from it and ignorance disappears through discrimination between Self and non-Self. Then appears the true self-effulgent knowledge of the oneness of God and Self.

'The discarding of the beginningless ignorance with its cause and effects and bodies and states, is like the ending of the beginningless non-existence, or the ending of a dream when the waking state supervenes. Liberation from the bondage of the false ego concept can never come about except through knowledge acquired by discrimination between the Self and the non-Self. Therefore you also must discriminate in order to remove the non-existent ego. Even this intellectual sheath is subject to change, insentient, a part of a whole, and an object of perception and therefore it cannot be the *ātman*. Can the non-eternal ever become eternal?

'Coming now to the sheath of Bliss: this is only a modification of ignorance on which the supreme Self is reflected. It reveals itself at will in all three states, waking, dreaming, and deep sleep, and yields the different modes of bliss from perceiving, obtaining, and experiencing things. It is experienced effortlessly by all to some extent in deep sleep, but sadhus who have practised discrimination, experience the bliss of it perpetually without effort and its fullness in the deep sleep state. However, even this sheath of bliss cannot be the supreme Self, since it is subject to change and possesses attributes. It is the effect of past good deeds and a modification of *prakriti* and it abides in the other sheaths which are themselves also modifications. If, by the rejection of false ideas, all five sheaths are eliminated, the Self alone is experienced as "I-I". It alone remains, whole and Self-aware, distinct from the five sheaths, the witness of the three states, self-effulgent, immutable, untainted, everlasting Bliss. It is like Devadatta[2] who neither is the pot nor partakes of its nature but is only the witness. The Self is not the five sheaths, which are objects, nor does it partake of their nature, but is a mere witness of them.'

To this the disciple replies: 'Oh Master, after rejecting the five sheaths as unreal, I find nothing remaining except the void, so what is there to be known as "I-I", as the truth of the Self?'

The Guru replies: 'Oh learned one, you are skilful in discrimination and have spoken the truth. The rule of enquiry or perception is: "That which is perceived by something else has the latter for its witness. When there is no agent of perception there can be no question of the thing having been perceived at all." Accordingly, the Self, as awareness, cognizes not only itself but also the existence of the ego with its various modifications of the transient names and forms and their nescience. Therefore it is the Self which is their witness. Beyond it there is nothing to know. It is aware of itself through its own effulgence and so is its own witness. It is single and immutable in the waking, dream, and deep sleep states. It makes itself known as Being-Consciousness-Bliss and is self-effulgent in the heart as "I-I". Through your keen intellect, know this eternal blissful awareness to be the Self or "I". The fool takes the reflection of the sun in the water of a pot to be the sun; the wise man eliminates pot, water, and reflection and knows the sun in the sky as it really is, single and unaffected, but illuminating all three. In the same way the fool, through error and misperception, identifies himself with the ego and its reflected light experienced through the medium of the intellect. The wise and discriminating man eliminates body, intellect, and reflected light of consciousness, and probes deeply into his real Self which illuminates all three, while remaining uniform in the ether of the heart. Thereby he realizes the eternal witness which is absolute knowledge, illuminating all. It is subtle and all-pervasive, neither being nor non-being, with neither inside nor outside, and is self-effulgent. Realizing this, he is set free from the impurities of the ego. He has no more birth or death. He is free from sorrow and becomes the immutable essence of established Bliss. The *jnāni* who, through experience, has realized his Self to be the *Brahman* as it really is, as Truth, Knowledge, endless Bliss, the single essence, eternal, boundless, pure, unattached, and indivisible, not only does not return to bondage but is that *Brahman* itself, the *advaita*. That is to say that knowledge of the identity of *Brahman* and Self is the prime cause of release from bondage. For him who aspires after liberation there is no other way of release from bondage but knowledge of the identity of *Brahman* and Self. Therefore you too, by your own experience, know your Self as always, "I am *Brahman*", "*Brahman* am I", "*Brahman* alone am I".

'Since there is nothing other than *Brahman*, it is the supreme *advaita*. The pot which is made of clay, has no other form than that of the clay. No one can show the pot except by means of the clay. The pot is only a delusion of the imagination and exists only in name, since it has no other reality than that of the clay. Similarly the whole universe is a superimposition (of form) on the *Brahman* although it seems to be separate from it. The substratum of *Brahman* appears through the delusion of the superimposition. The latter is really non-existent, like the serpent seen in the rope. The manifest is only an illusion. The silver seen in the substratum of the mother-of-pearl has no existence apart from it but is the mother-of-pearl itself. Similarly, manifestation has no existence apart from its substratum of *Brahman*. Whatever, oh sadhu, appears to the deluded as the manifested world of names and forms, on account of their ignorance and wrong knowledge, whatever objectivity appears as real, all this, when truly realized as it is, is the effect of *Brahman*, and is superimposed on the substratum of *Brahman*. Only owing to delusion it appears to be real and it is *Brahman*, its substratum, which appears to be superimposed on it. Really all these names and forms are nothing at all. They are a myth pure and simple and have no existence apart from their substratum of *Brahman*. They are nothing but the Being-Consciousness-Bliss which neither rises nor sets. If it were contended that the manifested world has any existence apart from *Brahman*, that would impair the infinity of *Brahman*. It would also contradict the authority of the *Atharva Veda* which declares in unequivocal terms "All this world is indeed *Brahman*". It would also make out the omniscient Lord as having uttered a falsehood when He said: "All these elements are not in Me. I, the Indivisible Whole, am not in them". The *mahātmas*, who are true sadhus, would not countenance these contradictions. Furthermore, the outer world does not exist in the state of deep sleep, and, if investigated, it is seen to be unreal, like the dream world. Therefore any such statement made by fools as that the manifested world has its own existence apart from its substratum of *Brahman*, is as false as the idle words of a man talking in his sleep. It is *Brahman* itself which shines everywhere, uniform and complete. This truth the enlightened (*jnānis*) know as the One without a second, formless, inactive, unmanifest, never to be destroyed, having no beginning or end. It is Truth, absolute purity, the essence of pure Bliss. It contains none of the internal

differences which are the creation of *māyā*. It is eternal, continuous, immaculately pure, spotless, nameless, undifferentiated,
self-effulgent, beyond the triads of knower-knowledge-known,
absolute, pure, unbroken Consciousness, ever-shining.

'My beloved disciple, this Self can neither be held nor given
up. It is beyond perception and utterance. It is immeasurable
without beginning or end. This infinity of *Brahman* is my Self
and yours and that of other individuals. Great texts such as
"That thou art" reveal the identity between the *Brahman* known
as "That" and the individual known as "thou". The identity is
not shown by the literal meaning of "that" and "thou". The
literal meaning of "that" is *Ishvara*'s *māyā* which is the cause of
the universe, and the literal meaning of "thou" is the five
sheaths of the ego. These are non-existent superimpositions,
the cause and effect of non-existent phantoms. Their qualities
are opposite to each other, like the sun and the glow-worm, the
king and the slave, the ocean and the well, Mt. Meru and the
atom. There can be no identity between *Brahman* and the
individual in the literal sense of "that" and "thou", and it is not
in this way that the scriptures postulate the identity.

'[The science of the secondary meaning of words is called
lakshana and is of three kinds. The first is called *jaha-ajahal-
lakshana*. In the first, the primary sense of a term is rejected and
the secondary retained; in the second, the primary sense is
retained and the secondary rejected; in the third, the primary
sense is only partly rejected and partly retained.][3] Of these three,
we can omit the first two as being of no use for our purpose and
take the third. According to this, in a text such as "He is that
Devadatta" we eliminate the contradictory aspects of Devadatta
manifested at different places and times, and concentrate on the
identity of Devadatta himself irrespective of place and time.
Similarly, in the text in question, we eliminate the non-existent,
objective, contradictory attributes of "that" and "thou" as "not

this, not this" (am I). You can do this on the authority of the Vedas which reject the duality superimposed on *Brahman*, and also by your own intelligence. If attributes such as a shield for a royal person and a badge of ownership for a slave are removed, both alike belong to the genus man. Similarly the text (about "that" and "thou") declares the natural identity between *Ishvara* and the individual in their residuary aspect of Consciousness apart from the forms of *Isvara* and individual. There is no contradiction in this, since Consciousness is the unbroken, single essence of both. Through the touch of the *mahātmas*, know this blessed identity of *Brahman* and Self by rejecting as "not I" the non-existent body. Know by your own clear intellect that *Brahman* is your Self, self-existent, subtle as the ether, ever radiant, true, awareness, bliss, indivisible and whole.

'Truly "thou art That", the Self that is non-dual *Brahman*, pure and exquisitely serene, the Truth apart from which nothing is. This is so because, even in this waking state, the world and the body with its sense and the ego which, owing to ignorance, seems to be separate from the Self, and the life breath are pure myth. "Thou art That" because in the dream state, time, space and objects and the knower of them are all created by sleep and are purely illusory. "Thou art That" because this whole world emanates from *Brahman*, which alone IS, and is *Brahman* itself, just as pots come from clay and are clay itself and indeed are made of clay. That *Brahman* is untouched by the six-fold changes of birth, youth, growth, old age, decay, and death. It has not caste or custom, tribe or family, name or form. It is without attributes. It has neither merit nor demerit, neither mental nor physical afflictions. It is free from the six evils of hunger, thirst, sorrow, delusion, old age and death. It has no time, space or objectivity. It cannot be described by words. The gross mind cannot reach it. It can be comprehended only by the eye of wisdom and experienced in the heart of the yogi, in his very being, not by the

use of any organ. It is the substratum of the illusory world that
seems to be superimposed on it. It is the cause of the emanation,
preservation, and re-absorption of the world. It is the supreme
cause, which itself has no cause; all the worlds of name and form
are its effects, and yet it is distinct from cause and effect. It is
distinct from being and non-being. Although, owing to delusion,
it appears like gold in its varying aspects of name and form and
its modifications, yet it has no name or form, no attributes or
modifications. It contains no disequilibrium. It is still, like a
waveless ocean. It is eternal, formless, spotless, incomparable,
ever free, indestructible, pure, without beginning. It is that
beyond which there is nothing. It is complete, not compounded
of elements or of parts. It is Being-Consciousness-Bliss,
uniform, indivisible Bliss. It is single in essence. That *Brahman*
which is all this, "That thou art". Meditate on the truth of this
in your heart continuously, without break, calmly, with reason
and keen intellect. Thus you will obtain essential knowledge free
from doubt, as clear as water in the palm of the hand. Knowledge
in the body with its faculties is like a king in the midst of his vast
army, and that knowledge is the Self and is *Brahman*. Know this
by discrimination. Regard all other separate things as This Itself
and remain ever as this Self. Thus remaining, you will attain Bliss
and peace of Being.

'In the cavity of the intellect is the single truth of *Brahman*,
distinct from being and non-being. He who remains eternally as
that Truth itself is never drawn back again to birth in the body.

'Although a man knows this to be true, the feeling of "I am
the doer", "I am the enjoyer" arises strongly in him owing to the
bondage (*samsāra*) caused by the mighty, beginningless *vāsanās*
(innate tendencies) which often obstruct him. Curb these
tendencies the moment they arise, by your own efforts, by
abiding firmly in the Self, by a vision of the Self. Sages such as
Vasishta have declared that the withering of the *vāsanās* is indeed

liberation. Realization of the Self as it is does not come through tendencies to worldly or sense activity or through prolonged study of the scriptures. To those who seek deliverance from the prison or ocean of *samsāra*, the above threefold tendencies are iron fetters say those who are realized. Therefore attachment to the world, the scriptures, and the body must be given up and it must be fully realized that the body is sustained by the force of *prārabdha* (past *karma*). You should, therefore, courageously renounce these attachments and strive energetically to overcome *tamas* by the power of *sattva* and *rajas*, then *rajas* through mixed *sattva*, then mixed *sattva* through pure *sattva*. You should do this with a firm and calm mind, helped by the great texts such as "That thou art" which proclaim the identity between the individual self and *Brahman*. Seek by reasoning and experience to get rid of the *vāsanās*, so that you may have firm faith in *Brahman* and completely root out from the body and senses the feeling of "I" and "mine" which constantly appears as a result of the superimposition. This is to be done by firm abidance in the one indivisible Self in the Heart and by meditating on the unceasing experience of knowledge of the unity of *Brahman* and Self thus: "I am not the ego. I am the unceasing perfection of *Brahman* experienced as I, the witness of thought-forms." This meditation must be persisted in until the ego sense is completely rooted out from the body, without a vestige, and the world of individuals appears like a dream. He who mediates has no work to do except beg and perform his natural functions. He must never forget the Self by giving room for worldly speech and sense objects. Sandalwood is fragrant by nature, but its fragrance is masked by a bad smell when it comes into contact with water and is revealed when it is rubbed. Constant practice of meditation is this rubbing. The latent tendencies of the mind are removed, only to the extent to which it abides in the Self. It is by such constant abidance in the Self that the mind of the yogi is destroyed. And by the destruction of the mind the outer non-self tendencies of the heart are utterly eradicated. Then the experience of the supreme Self, which was formerly veiled by the magic of the *vāsanās*, shines forth of its own accord like the fragrance of uncontaminated sandal-paste.

'In whatever way it may be examined, the ego with all its faculties turns out to be unreal, a momentary limitation, inert, insentient and incapable of realizing the One. The supreme Self is different from both gross and subtle bodies. It is the witness of the ego with its faculties and exists always, even in deep sleep. The texts say: "It is birthless and deathless." It is immutable and distinct alike from being and non-being. The ego can never be the real Self, the true meaning of "I". Keep aloof from this impure body as you would from an outcaste. Give up the sense of "I" in the gross body and all attachment due to the mind, attachments to name and form, tribe and family, caste and social order. Give up also the attachment to the subtle body and its nature and sense of being the doer. Find the feeling of "I" in the Self, which is Truth, knowledge, and eternity. Just as the air in a pot is part of the air outside, so conceive of the Self as that self-effulgent *Brahman* which is the substratum of all, in which the world is seen reflected like a city in a mirror or like shadows cast. Think of yourself as "That I am", without parts, without form, without activity, without duality, unending, Being-Conscious-ness-Bliss. Know the Self as it really is, Give up this false physical self just as an actor gives up his role and remains himself. By knowledge acquired through Self-enquiry discard both microcosm and macrocosm as unreal and, abiding in the unbroken stillness, remain ever at rest in the perfect Bliss as unqualified *Brahman*. Thus obtain supreme peace, which is the purpose of life.

'Though various obstacles contribute to the bondage of the soul, the primary cause of them all is the rising of the false ego-sense. It is through the superimposition of the ego on the Self that this bondage of birth, death and sorrow has come upon you who are by nature Being-Consciousness-Bliss, of boundless glory, eternal, single in essence, unchanging. By nature you have no such bondage. Just as there can be no sound health so long as the effect of a little poison in the body continues, so there can be no liberation so long as identification with the ego continues. Knowledge of the identity of the Self with *Brahman* is clearly revealed as soon as the ego is completely destroyed without residue, together with the illusion of multiplicity caused by the veiling of *tamas*. Therefore, by investigation into the nature of the unattached Self, discover the Truth of your own Self, complete, perfect, self-effulgent and ever-blissful. He who is freed from the ego shines eternally as the Self, like the full moon, radiant when delivered from the dragon's head (of eclipse). In the field of the heart the terrible cobra of the ego is coiled round the Bliss of the Self to which it denies access with the threefold hood of the *gunas*. These three fearful heads of the serpent of ego are to be severed, in accordance with the scriptures, only by great courage with the mighty sword of actual experience of the Self. He who has thus destroyed the three-hooded serpent can obtain and enjoy the vast treasure of the Bliss of *Brahman*. Therefore you, too, give up the I-sense in the ego, which appears like being and assumes that it is the doer, whereas it is only the reflected light of the Self. Turn inwards all the thought-forms that adhere to the ego. He is an enemy of yours, so kill him with the sword of knowledge. He has been harming you like a thorn in your throat while eating. Give up all desires in order to realize your state as the supreme Self. Enjoy the kingdom of the Self, be perfect, be still in the stillness of the immutable state of *Brahman*.

'The ego may in this way be killed, but if thought is given to it even for a moment it revives and engages in activity, driving a man before it as the wind drives winter clouds. Remember that he who associates the "I"-sense with the body and its faculties is bound while he who does not is liberated.

'Thoughts of sense objects create a sense of differentiation and thereby cause the bondage of birth and death. Therefore no quarter should be given to the ego, who is the enemy who has such thoughts. Just as a withered lime tree puts out new leaves if watered, so the ego revives through thoughts of sense objects. The increase of effects makes their seed or cause flourish, while the decay of effects destroys their cause also; therefore you should first destroy the effects. If thoughts, which are the effect, flourish, the ego with its tendencies, which is the cause, also flourishes. From thoughts, outer activities arise, and from these two together the tendencies develop and create the bondage to which souls are subject. In order to escape from this, thoughts, activity, and tendencies must all three be abolished. The best way of doing this is to hold firmly to the view that: "All this that appears as separate names and forms is *Brahman* itself." This view must be held to at all times and places and in all states. Firm holding to this attitude reduces activity, and this results in a decline of thoughts, which in turn destroys the latent tendencies. Destruction of the latent tendencies is indeed deliverance. Therefore develop this helpful tendency to regard everything as *Brahman*. The result will be that the frail tendencies of the ego will disappear like darkness before the sun. Just as darkness with all its dismal effects disappears before the rising sun, so bondage with all its sorrows will pass away without a trace when the sun of *advaitic* experience rises. Therefore regard all objective manifestation as *Brahman* and hold firm in a state of peace (*samādhi*) and inner and outer beatitude (*nischala bhāva*) as long as the bondage due to your past destiny (*karma*) lasts. While doing so, always remember: "That immovable Bliss of *Brahman* itself am I."

'This abidance as *Brahman* must never be relaxed, for if it is, a false notion of Truth will result which is indeed death, as says

Bhagavan Sri Sanatsujata, the son of Brahma. Such a false notion of truth due to swerving from the state of abidance in Truth introduces delusion; from delusion arises the attribution of "I" to the ego and its objects, from this bondage, and from bondage sorrow. Therefore there is no greater misfortune for the enlightened than wrong understanding and swerving from reality. Just as water-plants, though removed from a pool of water, do not stay at the side but cover it over again, so if a man is exteriorized, even though he may be enlightened, if *māyā* (illusion) once begins to shroud him he will be swayed in numerous ways by the false intellect. This is due to his lapse from watchfulness, his forgetting of his true state, his going out towards sense objects. He is like a man swayed and dominated by a lewd woman, of whom he is enamoured. If, through wrong understanding and swerving from reality, a man's consciousness slips even the least bit from the target of his own Self, it will enter into outer things and leap from one to another as a ball slips from your hand and rolls down a flight of stairs. It will begin to consider outer experiences good for it and thence will arise the desire to enjoy them. That will lead to participation in them, which in turn will destroy his abidance in the Self, with the result that he will sink into depths from which he can never more arise and will be destroyed. Therefore there is no greater danger in *Brahman*-consciousness than wrong understanding, which means swerving from one's true state. Only he who has the eternal state of consciousness (*nishtha*) obtains realization (*siddhi*) and so renounces the manifestation (*sankalpa*) born of *pramāda* (wrong understanding) and of relaxation from practice. Such wrong understanding is the cause of all spiritual decline (*aratha*). Therefore be the *swarupa nishtha* who abides ever in the Self.

'He who has attained liberation in the state of *Brahman* while still alive will shine so in his bodiless state also. It says in the Yajur Veda: "He who has even the slightest sense of differentiation is always afraid!" He who sees any attributes of differentiation, however small, in the absolute *Brahman*, will for that reason remain in a state of terror. He who locates the "I"-sense in the insentient body and its objects, so despised by the various scriptures and their commentaries, will experience sorrow after sorrow like the sinner who commits unlawful acts. We can see from the discrimination between thieves and honest men that he who is devoted to truth escapes misfortune and achieves success, while he who is devoted to falsehood perishes.[4] We also see that shutting out external objects gives the mind a clear perception of the Self, which in turn results in the destruction of the bondage of *samsāra*. Therefore the abandonment of all objective reality is the way to deliverance. If a man discriminates between Truth and non-truth in quest of liberation and discovers the Truth of the supreme Lord through the authority of the scriptures, will he then, like a child, run after non-existent chimera, knowing them to be the cause of his destruction? None would do so. Therefore he who discriminates must also renounce and cease to seek after externals which feed those lower tendencies that cause bondage. He should erase all sorrows due to ignorance by the experience "I am that supreme *Brahman* alone, which is Being-Consciousness-Bliss" and should abide ever in his true state, which is Bliss. One who is in the waking state is not dreaming and one who is in the dream state is not waking; the two are mutually exclusive. Similarly, one who is not attached to the body has deliverance and one who is has not.

'A liberated being is one who sees himself as single and the witness both within and without the world of things moving and unmoving, as the substratum of all. By his universal consciousness experienced through the subtle mind, he has removed all the vehicles and he remains as the absolute whole. Only such a one is liberated, and he has no attachment to the body. There is no other means of liberation than this blessed realization that "All is one Self". And this "All is one" attitude is to be obtained by perpetual abidance in the Self and rejection of objects without attachment to them. How can a man reject objective reality if he has the "I am the body" idea and is attached to outer things and always performing actions dictated by them? It is impossible. Therefore renounce all actions based on *karma* and *dharma* and, with knowledge of the *tattva*, abide permanently in the Self. Prepare your mind for immersion in perpetual Bliss. This effort will enable you to reject objective reality. It is in order to obtain this *sarvātmabhāva* (attitude that all is the Self) that the scriptural text "*Shānto dāntha*" (calm and self-controlled) prescribes *nirvikalpa samādhi* (ecstatic trance) for those seekers who have taken a vow of *chāndrāyana* (regulation of the increase and decrease of food intake through two successive fortnights) and have also performed *sravana* (hearing of the text "That thou art"). A scholar who has not had a firm experience of *nirvikalpa samādhi*, however learned he may be, will not be capable of destroying the ego and its objective reality together with all the accumulated tendencies of his previous births.

'It is the projecting power of *māyā* together with its veiling power which unites the soul with the ego, the cause of delusion, and, through its qualities, keeps a man vainly dangling like a ghost. If the veiling power is destroyed the Self will shine of itself, and there will be no room either for doubt or obstruction. Then the projecting power also will vanish, or even if it persists, its persistence will only be apparent. But the projecting power cannot disappear unless the veiling power does. Only when the subject is perfectly distinguished from objects, like milk from water, will the veiling power be destroyed.

'Pure discrimination born of perfect knowledge distinguishes the subject from the object and destroys the delusion due to ignorance. The man of discrimination distinguishes the real from the unreal, reasoning as follows: "Like iron combining with fire, the intellect combines with ignorance to obtain a fictitious unity with the Self which is Being, and projects itself as the world of seer, sight, and seen. Therefore all these appearances are false, like a delusion, dream, or imagination. All sense objects from the ego down to the body are also unreal, being modifications of *prakriti*, subject to change from moment to moment. Only the Self never changes. The Self, distinct from the body, distinct from being and non-being, the witness of the intellect and the meaning implied by the "I"-sense, single, eternal, indivisible, is indeed the supreme Self of eternal Bliss incarnate."

'In this way he discriminates between Truth and untruth and, in doing so, discovers the true Self. With the eye of illumination, he obtains actual realization of the Self and experiences this "I" as the indivisible knowledge of absolute *Brahman*. Thereby he destroys the veiling power and the false knowledge and other sorrows that have been created by the projecting power, just as the fear of a snake falls away as soon as one perceives the reality of the rope (that one took to be a snake). Being freed from these ills, he obtains abidance in a state of perfect peace. Thus, only when one obtains realization of the supreme identity through *nirvikalpa samādhi* will ignorance be destroyed without vestige and the knot of the heart loosed. How can there be any seed of *samsāra* still remaining in the liberated soul who has realized the supreme identity with the utter destruction of the forest of ignorance by the fire of knowledge of oneness of Self and *Brahman*? He has no more *samsāra*, no more rebirth and death. Therefore the discriminating soul must know the *ātma tattva* in order to be freed from the bondage of *samsāra*.

'All forms of creation and imagination appearing as you, I, this, etc, are a result of the impurity of the intellect. They seem to exist in the absolute, attributeless supreme Self, but in the state of absorption (*samādhi*) and experience of *Brahman* they cease to exist. Also the Self seems to be divisible owing to differences in the vehicles, but if these are removed it shines single and complete. Perpetual concentration is necessary in order to dissolve these differentiations in the Absolute. The wasp's grub that renounces all activity and meditates constantly upon the wasp becomes a wasp, and in the same way the soul that longs for *Brahman* with one-pointed meditation becomes the supreme Self through the power of its meditation and perpetual abidance in *Brahman*, in the absolute stillness. So persevere constantly in meditation on *Brahman*, and as a result the mind will be cleansed of the stain of the three *gunas* until it becomes perfectly pure and resumes its state, when it is ripe for dissolution in *Brahman* like salt in water. It is like gold being cleansed of its alloy and returning to the purity of its true state through being put in a furnace. Only in such purity of mind can *nirvikalpa samādhi* be obtained, and therewith the essential bliss of identity. Through this *samādhi* all the knots of the *vāsanās* are loosened and all past *karmas* destroyed so that the Light of the Self is experienced without effort, inwardly and outwardly, and at all places and times. Thus the subtle *Brahman* is experienced in the single mental mode of *samādhi* by those of subtle intellect, and in no other way, by no gross outlook, can it be experienced. Similarly the sage who has inner and outer senses controlled, in solitude and equanimity, obtains experience of the all-pervading Self through perpetual concentration and thus, getting rid of all mental creations caused by the darkness of ignorance, becomes actionless and without attributes and remains eternally in the Bliss of *Brahman* himself. Only he is liberated from the bondage of *samsāra* who, having obtained *nirvikalpa samādhi*, perceives the mind, senses, and objects, the ears and sound, etc, to inhere in the Self, and not he who speaks only from theoretical wisdom. *Brahman* can be clearly experienced without any barrier only through *nirvikalpa samādhi*, for apart from that the mental mode always fluctuates, leading from one thought to another. Therefore control the senses and mind and abide firmly in the Self. Utterly destroy the darkness of ignorance and its cause through experience of the one Self and abide ever as the Self. Reflection on truth heard is a hundred times more potent than hearing it, and abiding in it is a hundred thousand times more potent than reflection on it. What limit, then, can there be to the potency obtained through *nirvikalpa samādhi*?

'Restraint of speech, not accepting anything from others, conquest of desire, renunciation of action, continence, and solitude are all aids in the early stages of this *samādhi* yoga. Solitude helps to quieten the senses, and thereby the mind also. Stillness of mind destroys the tendencies and thereby gives perpetual experience of the essential Bliss of *Brahman*. Therefore the yogi must always exert himself to restrain the mind. The breathing must subside into the mind, the mind into the intellect, the intellect into the witness, and by knowing the witness as the fulness of the unqualified supreme Self perfect peace is obtained.

'He who meditates becomes that aspect of his being to which the consciousness is drawn: if to the body, he becomes body, if to the senses he becomes senses, if to the life-breath, he becomes that, if to the mind or intellect, he becomes mind or intellect. Therefore, rejecting all these, the consciousness should subside and obtain peace in *Brahman*, which is eternal Bliss.

'He who, through desire for Liberation, has attained perfect freedom from desires is able to abide in the Self and get rid of all attachments, inner as well as outer, and he alone achieves inner and outer renunciation. Moreover, it is only he who is without desires, who has perfect non-attachment and so obtains *samādhi* and through *samādhi* the certainty that he has won to *tattva jnāna*, which brings liberation. He who has attained liberation has attained eternal Bliss. Therefore complete non-attachment is the only path for him who aspires to the bliss of union with the bride of liberation. Non-attachment combined with Self-knowledge wins the kingdom of deliverance. Non-attachment and knowledge are like the wings of a bird needed for ascending the mount of deliverance, and if either of them is lacking it cannot be attained. Therefore renounce the desire for things, which is like poison; give up attachment to caste, group, social position, and destiny; cease to locate the "I"-sense in the body; be ever centred upon the Self; for in truth you are the witness, the stainless *Brahman*.

'The Self in the form of *Brahman*, witness of all finite beings, self-effulgent, shines eternally as "I-I" in the sheath of *Vijnāna*, distinct from the five sheaths. Being experienced as "I", it shines as the true form of the Self, the direct experience of the great texts. Fix your heart constantly on this *Brahman*, which is the goal. Let the senses remain in their centres; keep the body steady by remaining indifferent to it; and practise the meditation "I am *Brahman*, *Brahman* am I", allowing no other thoughts to come in. Gradually still the mind by practice of the unbroken flow of beatitude. Realize the identity of Self and *Brahman* and drink the nectar of *Brahman* Bliss in eternal joy. What use are base thoughts of body and world, which are non-Self? Give up these non-Self thoughts, which are the cause of all sorrow. Hold firm to the Self, the seat of Bliss, as "I" and no longer ascribe the "I"-sense to the ego and its attributes. Be absolutely indifferent to them and meditate perpetually on the Self, which is the cause of liberation.

'A pot, a huge earthen jar for storing grain, and a needle are all separate things, but when they are cast away there remains only the single expanse of ether. Something which is falsely imagined to exist on the substratum of something else has no reality apart from the real thing, just as a snake imagined in a piece of rope has not. Wave, foam, bubble, and whirlpool if examined are all found to be simply water. Pots of various sizes and shapes are nothing other than clay, and in fact are clay. Similarly, you should reject the limitations of body, senses, life-breath, mind, and ego, which are merely illusory. Only fools perceive and speak of "I", "you", "it" and so forth out of delusion and folly, being drunk with the wine of illusion (*māyā*). Even their perception of multiplicity is contained in Being-Consciousness-Bliss, in the perfect purity of Self which, as *Brahman*, shines as one indivisible whole, like the vast ether. All superimpositions such as body and ego-sense, from *Brahman* down to a boulder, which are perceived as the world, are really nothing other than the one Self. They are merely the display of *prakriti* and the Self as pure Being. The one supreme Self, unbroken and homogeneous, exists as east, west, south, and north, inner and outer, up and down, everywhere. He himself is Brahma; he himself is Vishnu, Siva, Indra, gods and men, and everything. What more is there to say? Everything from (the threefold appearance of) personal God, individual beings, and world down to the minutest atom is merely a form of *Brahman*. In order to remove the superimposition of *mithya* (the false), the scriptures declare "there is no duality at all" (*Brahman* is one without a second); therefore you yourself are the non-dual *Brahman*, spotless like the ether, without inner or outer, without attributes, changeless, timeless, without dimensions or parts. What else is there to know? The scriptures declare: "So long as the individual regards the corpse of his body as 'I' he is impure and subject to various ills such as birth, death and sickness," "Remove all objective reality superimposed on the Self by illusion and know yourself as pure, immutable Siva; then you will become liberated, the *Brahman* which is without action and is indivisible perfection." The enlightened who have attained supreme knowledge shine as Being-Consciousness-Bliss, homogeneous *Brahman*, having utterly renounced objective reality. Therefore you, too, reject your gross, impure body and the subtle body that wavers like the wind and the "I"-sense in them and regard yourself as Being-Consciousness-Bliss, as declared by

Vēdānta, and thus remain forever as the very *Brahman*.

'The scriptures declare that: "Duality is of the nature of illusion (*māyā*) and only non-duality is the Supreme Truth." It is our experience that the diversity created by the consciousness ceases to exist in deep sleep, in which the consciousness is absorbed in bliss. Those who are wise and discriminating know that the proverbial serpent has no existence apart from the substratum of the rope, nor the water of a mirage apart from the barren ground. It is our experience that when the mentality assumes the nature of the Self and becomes one with the attributeless supreme Self, mental manifestation ceases. All these magical creations which the illusion of the mind sets forth as the universe are found to have no real existence and become untrue when the Truth behind them is realized as *Brahman* itself. In the non-dual *Brahman* the threefold reality of seer, sight, and seen does not exist. It is the substratum into which ignorance, the root cause of the illusion of multiplicity, is absorbed, like darkness into light. Like oceans that endure to the end of the cycle of time, the Truth of *Brahman* remains single, complete, absolute purity, inactivity, unqualified, changeless, formless. Where, then, can be talk of duality or diversity in the homogeneity of *Brahman*? When in a state of *samādhi*, the enlightened *jnāni* experiences in the heart as "I-I" the homogeneous completeness of that *Brahman* which is eternal, the bliss of knowledge incomparable, unattached, formless, inactive, unqualified, immutable, characterless, nameless, and free from bondage. It is still, like the ether − and yet nothing can be compared to it. It has no cause and is not an effect. It is beyond imagining. It is to be achieved only through realization on the authority of the *Vēdānta*. The truth of it abides in the heart and is experienced constantly as I. It is free from birth, old age, and death. In itself it is eternal. It is eternal, tranquil, and undifferentiated; it is vast and still like a calm ocean without a shore. In order not to fall back into *samsāra*, practise *nirvikalpa samādhi* by concentration on *Brahman*, which is experienced in the heart as our own radiant Self free from all limitations and as Being-Consciousness-Bliss. This will destroy the individual consciousness which is the cause of all error, and thus you can unravel the knot of the heart which causes the ills of birth and death. Thus will you obtain the glory of unbroken bliss, being Self-realized, and by doing so achieve the purpose of human life, a boon so rare to obtain.

'The Self-realized yogi, knowing his true nature, the great *mahātma*, shows his wisdom by rejecting his body, regarding it as a corpse, as the mere shadow of his being, existing only owing to past destiny. Such a great *mahātma* knows himself to be the unbroken bliss of the Self. He has utterly consumed the body and its attributes in the fire of *Brahman*, which is eternal, immutable Truth. Having thus consumed his body and remaining with his consciousness ever immersed in the ocean of bliss which is *Brahman*, he himself is eternal Knowledge and Bliss. How then should he care to nourish or sustain his body or be attached to it, feeding as he does on the eternal nectar of *Brahman*, inwardly and outwardly? Just as the cow does not care about the garland round its neck, so too he does not care whether the body, bound by the strings of past *karma*, lives or dies. So you too reject this inert, impure body and realize the pure and eternal Self of wisdom. Give no more thought to the body. Who would care to take back what he has once vomited?

'Knowledge of a mirage keeps one away from it, and ignorance that it is a mirage leads one to seek it. Similarly, knowledge leads to the path of release and ignorance leads to worldly pursuits. The achievement of Self-knowledge or Self-realization frees a man from the ills arising from error and brings him eternal contentedness and unequalled bliss eternally experienced; ignorance, on the other hand, pushes him into objective experience of error and misery. How then should the wise man, who has severed the knot of the heart with the sword of wisdom, continue to perform the various vain actions which occupied him during the time of his delusion? What cause could induce him to activity?

'Knowledge leads to non-attachment; solitude and abandonment of home lead to knowledge; the bliss of Self-experience and tranquillity results from cessation of activity. If these results are not obtained step by step, the previous steps become invalid. The perfection of non-attachment is when previous tendencies to seek enjoyment no longer arise. The perfection of knowledge is when the "I"-sense no longer pertains to the body. The perfection of solitude is when thoughts subside through perpetual striving and, dissolving in *Brahman*, no longer turn outwards.

'Do not differentiate between Self and *Brahman* or between world and *Brahman*. On the authority of the Vedas realize "I am *Brahman*". Attain the pure beatitude of oneness and establish the pure consciousness immovably in *Brahman* so that you become dissolved in *Brahman*. Being ever *Brahman*, renounce objective reality and let your enjoyments be witnessed or known by others, like the state of sleeping children. Renounce activity and, with the purity of primal Beings, abide in eternal enjoyment of pure Bliss. Although your mind is dissolved and you are like one forgetful of the world, remain ever awake, and yet like one who is not awake. Remain indifferent to the body and senses and outer things that follow you like a shadow. Be one who discriminates, free from the stain of *samsāra* and from tendencies and sense objects. Retain consciousness without thought. Retain form, though formless. Have no likes and dislikes in what is experienced at the moment and no thought of what may happened in the future. Give up all thought of inner and outer and concentrate permanently on the blissful experience of *Brahman*. Through the power of knowledge maintain perfect equanimity in the face of all opposites such as vice and virtue, likes and dislikes, or praise and blame whether by sadhus or by the wicked. The dedicated sage is like a river emptied into the ocean, untouched by the attack of sense objects, absorbed in the Self, and it is only such a one who attains realization while still in the body. He alone is worshipful and reaps the reward of worthy actions. All his innate tendencies have been destroyed by his knowledge of identity with *Brahman* and no renewal of *samsāra* can be ascribed to him. Just as even the most lustful person never thinks of enjoying his own mother, so the sage who experiences the perfection of *Brahman* never turns back to *samsāra*. If he does, then he is not a sage who has known *Brahman* but only an outward-turning fool.

'Identity with *Brahman* is the fire of knowledge which burns up *sanchita karma* (destiny stored up for future lives) and *āgāmi karma* (destiny being created in this life). *Sanchita karma* is destroyed because it can no longer cause birth in higher or lower worlds once the sage has awakened from the illusion of activity in which he harvested merit and demerit through countless ages. And *āgāmi karma* can no longer affect him because he knows himself to be established as the supreme *Brahman*, indifferent as the ether to the effects of *karma*. There is ether in a pot containing alcohol, but is it affected by the smell of the alcohol? Not at all. Having spoken of the *sanchita* and *āgāmi karma* of the sage, it now remains to explain how his *prārabdha karma* (that part of past *karma* which is to be experienced in this life) is also a myth. Although ever absorbed in his true state, he is sometimes seen to experience the fruits of his past actions or to take part in outer activity; so people say that he is not free from *karma* since he must reap the good and bad effects of past action. Does not the rule that there is fruit of past action where there is destiny and no fruit where there is no destiny apply to the sage also? They argue: if one shoots an arrow at an animal, thinking it to be a tiger, but it later turns out to be a cow, can the arrow be recalled? Once shot, it will certainly have to kill the cow. So too, they say, destiny that started on its course prior to the dawn of enlightenment must produce its effects, so that the sage is still subject to *prārabdha karma* only and must experience its effects. However, the scriptures declare such *prārabdha* to be unreal, because a man who has awakened from a dream experience does not go back into the same dream, or desire to cling to the dream experiences or the body and environment of the dream as "I" and "mine". He is perfectly free from the dream world and happy in his awakened state, whereas a man who retains any attachment to the dream cannot be said to have left the state of sleep. In the same way, one who has realized the identity of *Brahman* and Self sees nothing else. He eats and excretes but as though in a dream. He is beyond all limitations and associations. He is the absolute *Brahman* itself. The three kinds of *karma* do not affect him in the least, so how can one say that only *prārabdha karma* affects him? Is one who has awakened still dreaming? Even if it were said that *prārabdha karma* affects the sage's body, which has been constructed from the result of past *karma*, that would only affect him so long as he had the "I am the body" idea, but once that is gone, *prārabdha* cannot be attributed to him, since he is the Self, not born of *karma*, beginningless, pure, and described by the scriptures as "unborn, eternal, and deathless". But to attribute *prārabdha* to the body, which is unreal and a figment of illusion, is itself an illusion. How can an illusion be born, live, and die as reality? It may be asked why, then, should the scriptures refer to a non-existent *prārabdha*? It may also be asked how the body can continue to exist through knowledge after the death of ignorance and its effects. To those who are so misguided and under the influence of false ideas, the explanation is given that the scriptures admit that the sage has illusory *prārabdha* only as a concession for the sake of argument and not to postulate that the sage has a body and faculties. In him is visible the eternally established state of non-dual *Brahman*, beyond mental or verbal

description and definition, without beginning or end, integral
Being-Consciousness-Bliss, stabilized, homogeneous, never to
be rejected or obtained, subtle, inwardly and outwardly complete,
with no substratum, beyond the *gunas*, without colour, form, or
change, as pure Being. Nothing at all is to be seen there of what
obtains here. It is only by knowledge of this oneness in the heart
through *ātma yoga*, by renouncing enjoyment and the very desire
for enjoyment, that dedicated sages who have peace and self-
control obtain supreme deliverance.

'Therefore, my son, if you too, by the eye of wisdom obtained
through unwavering *samādhi*, discover beyond all doubt the
supreme Self or perfect bliss which is your original nature, you
will no longer have any doubts about what you have heard. Cast
out, therefore, the delusion created by the mind and become a
sage, a realized man who has attained the purpose of life. The
teacher, like the scriptures, gives instructions common to all, but
each person must experience bondage and deliverance, hunger
and satisfaction, sickness and health for himself; others can only
infer it from him. Similarly, he who discriminates must cross the
ocean of birth and death by his own efforts through the grace of
the supreme Lord. Thus obtaining release from bondage, which
is due only to ignorance, remain as Being-Consciousness-Bliss.
The scriptures, reason, the words of the guru, and inner experience are the means you have to use for this.

'The essence of the *Vēdāntic* scriptures may be condensed into
the following points.

'First: In me, the unmoving *Brahman*, all that seems different
is utterly without reality. I alone am. This is called the
standpoint of elimination (*bādha drishti*).

'Second: The dream and all else that appears in me as the
result of magic is an illusion. I alone am the Truth. This is called
the standpoint of illusion (*mithyā drishti*).

'Third: All that appears as form apart from the sea, that is the bubble and the wave, is the sea. All that is seen in a dream is seen in him who sees the dream. Similarly, in me as in the ocean or the man who dreams, all that seems separate from me is myself. This is called the standpoint of resolving (the effect into its cause) (*pravilāpa drishti*).

'Reject the outer world by any of these three means and recognize him who sees it to be infinite, pure, homogeneous *Brahman*, who is the Self. He who has thus realized *Brahman* is liberated. Although all three of these viewpoints are aids to realization, the third, in which one conceives everything as one's own Self, is the most powerful. Therefore, knowing the indivisible Self to be one's own Self, by one's own experience, one must abide in one's own true nature, beyond any mental form. What more is there to say? The whole world and all individuals are really *Brahman*, and abidance as that indivisible *Brahman* is itself deliverance. This is the essence and conclusion of all the Vedas. The scriptures are the authority for this.'

The disciple realized the truth of the Self through these words of the Guru, through the authority of the scriptures and by his own understanding. He controlled his sense organs and, becoming one-pointed, remained for a short time absorbed in unswerving *samādhi* in that supreme Self. Then he rose up and spoke thus to his Guru:

'Oh Master of the supreme experience, incarnation of the supreme peace, of *Brahman*, of the eternal essence of non-duality, endless ocean of grace, I bow down to you.'

Then, prostrating, he begins to tell of his own experience: 'Through the grace of the blessed sight of you the affliction due to the evil of birth is over and in an instant I have attained the blissful state of identity. By realization of the identity of *Brahman* and Self my feeling of duality has been destroyed and I am free from outer activity. I cannot discriminate between what is and what is not.[5] Like the iceberg in the ocean, I have become absorbed bit by bit into the ocean of the Bliss of *Brahman* until I have become that ocean itself, whose nature and extent my intellect fails to plumb. How can one conceive of the vastness of this ocean of Brahmic Bliss full of the divine essence, how to describe it in words? The word that was perceived a moment ago has entirely vanished. Where has it gone? By whom has it been removed? Into what has it been dissolved? What a wonder is this! In this vast ocean of Brahmic Bliss full of divine experience, what is there to reject or accept, to see, hear or know, apart from its own Self? I alone am the Self of Bliss. I am unattached; I have neither a gross nor a subtle body. I am indestructible; I am perfect stillness; I am neither the doer nor the enjoyer; I undergo no change. Action is not mine. I am not the seer or the hearer, the speaker, the doer, or the enjoyer. I am neither things experienced nor things not experienced but he who illumines both. I am the void, within and without. I am beyond compare. I am the spirit of old. I am without beginning. There is no creation in me of "I" or "you", or "this" or "that". I am both within and without all the elements as the conscious ether in them and also as the sub-stratum on which they are. I am Brahma, I am Vishnu, I am Rudra, I am Isa, I am Sadasiva. I am beyond *Ishvara*.[6] I am the all-comprehensive witness, the indivisible, homogeneous *Brahman*, infinite, eternal, being itself, unbroken whole perfection, exis-tence, eternal, pure, enlightened, liberated, and of supreme Bliss. What were formerly experienced as separate things and as experiencer-experience-experienced I now find to be all in myself. Even though the waves of the world arise owing to *māyā*, as a wind rises and subsides, they arise and subside in me who is the unbounded ocean of Bliss.

'Fools who are condemned for their errors wrongly ascribe body and other ideas to me who is formless and immutable. It is like dividing illimitable, formless time into parts such as year, half-year and season. Just as the earth is not made wet by the waves of mirage, so destruction cannot touch me in any way, for I am unattached like the ether, separate from all that I illumine, like the sun, motionless as a mountain, boundless as the ocean. Just as the ether is unaffected by the clouds, so am I by the body; how then can it be my nature to wake up, dream, and sleep, as the body does? It is only the bodily limitations (upon Being) that come and go, act and reap the fruits of action, that are born, exist, and dissolve. How can I perform *karma*, choose activity or withdrawal, reap the fruits of merit and demerit, I who am like the fixed mountain mentioned in the *Purānas*, who is ever motionless, indivisible, complete and perfect, like the ether, who is one perfect whole without senses, consciousness, form, or change? If a man's shadow is cold or hot or has good or evil qualities, that does not affect the man at all; and in the same way I am beyond virtues and vices. The scriptures also declare this. Just as the nature of a house does not affect the light within it, so too, objective characteristics cannot affect me who is their witness, distinct from them, changeless, and untouched. Just as the sun witnesses all activity, so am I the witness of this whole objective world. Just as fire pervades iron, so do I permeate and enlighten the world; and at the same time I am the substratum on which the word exists like the imaginary serpent in a piece of rope. Being the self-effulgent "I", I am not the doer of anything nor he who causes it to be done. I am not the eater nor he who causes anything to be eaten; I am not the seer nor he who causes anything to be seen.

'It is the superimposed adjunct that moves. This movement of the reflected consciousness is ascribed by the ignorant to the Consciousness itself. So too, they say that I am the doer, the enjoyer, that I, alas, am them. Being inactive like the sun (in causing growth upon the earth), being the Self of the forms and elements, I remain untouched by the reflected light of consciousness. It makes no difference to me if this body drops down on

earth or in water. The qualities of the reflected light of consciousness no more affect me than the shape of a pot affects the
ether inside it. States and functions of the intellect such as
doing, enjoying, understanding, being dull-witted or drunk,
bound or liberated, do not affect me since I am the pure non-
dual Self. The duties (*dharmas*) arising from *prakriti* in their
thousands and hundreds of thousands no more affect me than
the shadow cast by clouds affects the ether. I am that in which
the whole universe from *prakriti* down to gross matter appears as
a mere shadow, that which is the substratum, which illumines all,
which is the Self of all, is of all forms, is all pervasive and yet
distinct from all, that which is all void, which is distinct without
any of the attributes of *māyā*, that which is scarcely to be known
by the gross intellect, which is ether itself, which has neither
beginning nor end, which is subtle, motionless, formless,
inactive, immutable, that pure *Brahman* in its natural state,
unbroken, eternal, true, aware, endless, self-subsistent Bliss, non-
dual *Brahman*.

'Master, I was perplexed in the nightmare forest of *samsāra*, of
birth, old age, and death, caused by *māyā*, distressed by the
tormenting episodes in it and terrified by the tiger of the ego.
You awakened me from that nightmare by your grace and saved
me, bringing me supreme Bliss. Great Master! by the glory of
your grace even I have obtained the empire of real Being. I have
become blessed and have accomplished the purpose of this life.
Redeemed from the bondage of birth and death, I realize the
reality of my being, which is the entire ocean of Bliss. Oh, it is all
the glory of your grace, oh supreme Master! Obeisance again and
again to your blessed feet which, being in the form of the pure
bliss of consciousness, are seen as the whole of creation.
Obeisance for ever and ever!'

The supreme Master is thus addressed with jubilant heart by
the disciple who bows at his feet after realizing the truth of the

one Being, the supreme Bliss. He replies: 'Just as he who has eyes
has nothing to do but delight in forms, so he who knows *Brahman*
has no other satisfying use for his intellect than experience of the
Brahman reality. Who would care to look at a painted moon when
the full moon shines in all its splendour for our delight? No one
who has true knowledge can give up the essence to find delight in
what is unreal. There is neither satisfaction nor banishment of
sorrow in the experience of unreality; therefore a man must make
every effort to see with the eye of realization and with the mind
in a state of perfect peace to see his own Self as *Brahman*, as the
truth of non-duality shining as the Self of the whole universe.
He must meditate on this and concentrate ceaselessly on the
Self. Then he will enjoy unbroken experience of essential Bliss
and this alone will satisfy him. It is the intellect which causes
restlessness, appearing as a city in the clouds in the attributeless
whole of the conscious Self, and so the intellect must achieve
absolute stillness and this will give eternal bliss and serenity in
Brahman. When stillness and silence have been attained there will
be contentment and peace. Perfect silence free from latent
tendencies is the only means of experiencing eternal bliss for the
mahātma, for he who knows *Brahman*, who has realized Self and
experiences unbroken bliss.

'The sage who has thus realized the supreme *Brahman* will ever
delight in the Self with unobstructed thought-current. He
comes and goes, stands, sits, and lies down, performs whatever
actions he will, with no need to observe place, time, posture,
direction, rules of *yama*, or other stages of yoga, or positions for
concentration. What need is there for rules such as *yama* for
realizing one's Self? No external discipline is needed to know
one's Self as "I am *Brahman*", just as "Devadatta"[7] needs no outer
technique to know himself as such. This ever-existent Self shines
of its own accord when the mind is pure, just as a pot is naturally
seen when the eyesight is not defective. There is no need to

consider the purity of place or time for abiding in the Self. Just
as the world is illumined by the sun, so all the universes and the
Vedas, *Shāstras*, *Purānas*, and various elements are illumined by
Brahman, who is also consciously self-effulgent. How can this
Brahman be illumined by any low non-existent non-self? This
supreme Self is self-effulgent with manifold powers (*shakti*),
incapable of being known by anyone, and yet is experienced by
everyone as the "I-I" in the heart. It is in realizing this *ātman* that
the knower of *Brahman* is released from bondage, and when
released he knows the contentment of experiencing the essence
of eternal Bliss. This perfection of his beauty is beyond
imagining. He feels no happiness or sorrow on account of outer
conditions, whether agreeable or disagreeable, and has no likes or
dislikes. He accepts like a child all conditions that surround him
owing to the desires of others. Just as an innocent boy is
absorbed in his game without worrying about hunger, thirst, or
physical distress, so is the sage absorbed in the play of his own
Self without ego-consciousness and delights permanently in the
Self. Ascending in the chariot of his body, he who enjoys the
wide expanse of pure consciousness begs his food without any
thought or feeling of humiliation, drinks the water from rivers,
wraps himself in clothes that have not been washed or dried, or
in the bark of trees, or goes naked. No code or rule of conduct
binds him, for he is permanently free. Although sleeping on the
ground, like a child or madman, he remains ever fixed on *Vēdānta*.
Mother Earth is the flowery couch on which he lies. He sleeps
without fear in the forest or cemetery, for his sport and pleasure
are in *Brahman*. He who is the universal Self assumes at will
countless forms and has countless experiences. In one place he
behaves like an idiot, in another like a learned man, and in a third
like one deluded. Again, in one place he moves about as a man of
peace, in another as a king, in another as a beggar eating out of
his hand for want of a bowl. At one place he is seen to be adored,

at another decried. Thus he lives everywhere and the Truth behind him cannot be perceived by others. Although he has no riches he is eternally in bliss. Although others may not help him he is mighty in strength. Although he may not eat, he is eternally satisfied. He looks on all things with an equal eye. Though acting, it is not he who acts; though eating, it is not he who eats; though he has a body, he is bodiless. Though individualized, he is the One Indivisible whole. Knowing *Brahman* and liberated while yet in the body, he is not affected by likes and dislikes, joys and sorrows, auspicious and inauspicious things, natural to the common man who is attached to the body. Although the sun is never really caught by the dragon's head (in an eclipse), it seems to be, and fools who do not know the truth say: "Look! The sun is caught!" Similarly they say that he who knows *Brahman*, has a body, but that is their delusion, because although he seems to have a body he is in no way affected by it. The body of the liberated man, although free from bondage, exists in one place or another, like the sloughed skin of a snake. The body of a liberated man, like a log of wood tossed up and down by the current of a river, may sometimes be immersed in pleasure owing to his *prārabdha* but even though this is so, due to the effects of latent tendencies in *prārabdha*, as with the body of a worldly person, he still remains the witness in his state of inner silence, the hub of the wheel, free from desire and aversion and utterly indifferent. He neither attaches the senses to the objects that give pleasure nor detaches them. The fruits of his actions do not affect him in the slightest, since he is completely drunk with the unbroken experience of the nectar of bliss. He who knows *Brahman* is the absolute Self, the supreme Lord, with no need for special forms of meditation. Of this there is no doubt.

'He who knows *Brahman* has achieved the purpose of life and is eternally liberated as *Brahman*, even though living in the body and using its faculties. Indeed, he realizes the state of *Brahman* even with the destruction of the body and its adjuncts. It is like an actor on the stage who is the same individual whether he wears a mask or not. It makes no difference to a tree whether the place where its dead leaf falls is auspicious or not, whether it is a river, a canal, a street, or a temple of Siva. Similarly, it does not affect the sage where his body, already burnt in the fire of knowledge, is cast away. The Being-Consciousness-Bliss of the Self does not perish with the body, breath, intellect, and sense organs any more than a tree does with its leaves, flowers, and fruit. The scriptures also declare: "Only that which is finite and mutable can perish," and also: "The Self, which is established consciousness, is Truth and is imperishable." The sage is *Brahman* in the perfect Bliss of non-duality; he is established in Truth, which is *Brahman*. How then, can it matter where and when he sheds his body, which is a vehicle of skin, flesh, and impurities? Getting rid of the body, the staff, and the water-pot (of the mendicant) is not really liberation; liberation as understood by the sages really means loosing the knot of ignorance in the heart.

'Just as a stone, a tree, a straw, grain, a mat, pictures, a pot, and so on, when burned, are reduced to earth (from which they came), so the body and its sense organs, on being burnt in the fire of knowledge, become knowledge and are absorbed in *Brahman*, like darkness in the light of sun. When a pot is broken the space that was in it becomes one with space; so too when the limitation caused by the body and its adjuncts is removed, the sage realized during life, shines as *Brahman*, becoming absorbed in the *Brahman* he already was, like milk in milk, water in water, or oil in oil, and is radiant as the one supreme Self. Thus, when the sage who abides as *Brahman*, which is pure Being, obtains his disembodied absolute state he is never again reborn. How can there be rebirth for a sage who abides as *Brahman*, his body and its limitations burnt by the fire of knowledge, the identity of individual and Supreme? The existence of all that is either affirmed or denied in the one substratum of the indestructible, unattached, non-dual, absolute Self depends only on the mind, just as the appearance or disappearance of the imaginary snake in a piece of rope has no basis in reality. Bondage and liberation are creations of *māyā*, superimpositions upon the *Brahman* imagined by the mind without any existence in reality. It is a fool who blames the sun for his own blindness. It is impossible to argue that bondage (*samsāra*) is caused by the veiling power (*tamas*) of *māyā* and liberation by its destruction, since there is no differentiation in the Self. Such an argument would lead to a denial of the truth of non-duality and an affirmation of duality. This would be contrary to the authority of the scriptures. How can there be any display of *māyā* in non-dual *Brahman*, which is perfect stillness, one whole like the ether, spotless, actionless, unstained, and formless? The scriptures even proclaim aloud: "There is in truth no creation and no destruction; no one is bound, no one is seeking liberation, no one is on the way to deliverance. There are none liberated. This is the absolute truth." My dear disciple, this, the sum and substance of all the Upanishads, the secret of secrets, is my instruction to you. You also may impart it to one who aspires after liberation, only be careful to examine him several times to make sure that he has real detachment and is free from all the sins and impurities of this dark age.'

On hearing these words from the Guru, the disciple bows down to him several times and then takes leave and goes home in a state of Bliss. The Master also, immersed in the ocean of Bliss, wanders about the land in order to purify it.

Thus has been revealed the true nature of the Self in the form of a dialogue between the Guru and his disciple, as any who seek liberation can easily understand. May these useful instructions be followed by those who have faith in the authority of the scriptures and who aspire after liberation, by those advanced seekers who perform their prescribed duties without caring for the fruits of their actions and have thus cleansed themselves of mental impurities, who are not attached to the comforts of *samsāra* and who have attained a state of equanimity.

Souls wandering about in the wild and terrible forest of *samsāra* are oppressed by the torment of thirst caused by the terrific heat of the threefold evil,[8] and are then deluded by the mirage of water. The great Master Shankara Bhagavath Padacharya wishes to inform them of the existence close at hand of an ocean of sweet water, the bliss of non-duality, so that they may obtain relief, and has blessed them with his Vivēkachūdāmani, 'the Crown Gem of Discrimination' which will confer on them the eternal bliss of liberation. This is beyond doubt.

Om

Peace, Peace, Peace.

MOST SIGNIFICANT VERSES

Selected by
Sri Bhagavan Ramana Maharshi

(Translator anon)

Of all the means to liberation, the greatest is devotion (*bhakti*). Devotion is defined as the investigation of one's true nature, or the investigation of the true nature of the Self.

The supreme Self, indicated directly (but not correctly represented) by the notion promoted by the word 'I', is the one Consciousness, eternal, indivisible and non-dual. It is the witness of the mind and other factors in the human personality. Neither being nor non-being in the empirical sense, it is a homogenous mass of bliss, the inmost reality.

Of the nature of pure Consciousness, different from nature and its modifications, illumining all this world and showing what does and what does not exist, itself without particular characteristics, the supreme Self shines throughout waking, dream and dreamless sleep, immediately evident as 'I', the witness of the mind.

Become aware of that which is present in your own heart as the Self. It manifests clearly within as the inmost self throughout waking, dream and dreamless sleep. It always asserts itself as 'I', 'I' in various forms. It assumes the ego-sense and so on, and assumes their various modifications. It manifests with the nature of eternal bliss and Consciousness.

Control your mind and obtain, through the radiance of your higher mind, immediate knowledge of your own true Self in yourself in the form "This I am". Cross over the shoreless ocean of worldly life with its waves of birth and death. Establish yourself in the Absolute and gain your highest end.

The Self is self-luminous. It is the Witness, ever shining within the sheath of the higher mind. Make this your goal, different in nature from the unreal. Identify yourself with it through inhibiting all differentiation in the mind.

One cannot apprehend the extremely subtle reality as the supreme Self through coarse worldly vision. It can only be known by noble souls of very subtle intellect through an extremely subtle modification of the mind brought about by yogic concentration (*Samādhi*).

When the mind, thus matured by constant practice, dissolves in the Absolute, there ensues a natural concentration, void of all false imagination, which brings immediate experience of the savour of non-dual bliss.

Through this concentration, there ensues the destruction of the whole knot of the subtle impressions and of all merit and demerit. Reality manifests effortlessly all the time, everywhere, on all sides, within and without.

The Absolute, the supreme non-dual principle, neither being nor non-being in the empirical sense, is present in the cave of the heart. He who dwells in that cave, identifying himself with That, never again enters the hovel of the body.

OM

DAKSHINĀMŪRTI STOTRA

Introduction by
Sri Bhagavan Ramana Maharshi

Brahman (the four-faced god) brought by his power of thought four sons, named Sanaka, Sananda, Sanatsujata and Sanatkumara. He asked them to attend to the work of creating the world, preserving it, etc, but they were not interested in it, being completely detached. They wandered about in search of peace and tranquillity. As they were extremely dispassionate and fit (to receive spiritual instruction) Siva, the great God of compassion, manifested himself before them in human form as Dakshināmūrti (god facing south) under a banyan tree. He sat silently absorbed in himself, his right hand showing the gesture known as *chinmudra*.[1] The four seekers were drawn to him even as iron is drawn to a magnet. They sat before him absorbed like him in the Self. Even advanced spiritual aspirants cannot easily understand this state of silence. The world, the seer and the awareness which enables it to be cognized stand as obstacles in their way. But since it is the single power (*Shakti*) which manifests itself as these three and again withdraws them into itself, everything is that power which is the Self. Shankaracharya has expounded this truth in the following hymn.

SHANKARACHARYA'S HYMN TO DAKSHINĀMŪRTI

(Translated from Sri Bhagavan's Tamil rendering)

According to Hindu legends, Dakshināmūrti (which means 'southward-facing') is God or Siva manifested as a youth who is the divine Guru and guides disciples older than himself through silent influence on their Heart. The name is also divided as Dakshinā-amūrti and taken to mean 'formless power'.

The Maharshi was Siva manifested, the divine Guru who taught, through silence and was therefore identified with Dakshināmūrti.

Invocation

That Shankara who appeared as Dakshināmūrti to grant peace to the great ascetics (Sanaka, Sananda, Sanatkumara and Sanatsujata), who revealed his real state of silence, and who has expressed the nature of the Self in this hymn, abides in me.

The Hymn

He who teaches through silence the nature of the supreme *Brahman*, who is a youth, who is the most eminent Guru surrounded by the most competent disciples that remain steadfast in *Brahman*, who has the hand-pose indicating illumination,[2] who is of the nature of bliss, who revels in himself, who has a benign countenance — that Father who has a south-facing form,[3] we adore.

To him who by *māyā*, as by dream, sees within himself the universe which is inside him, like a city that appears in a mirror, (but) which is manifested as if externally to him who apprehends, at the time of awakening, his own single Self, to him, the primal Guru, Dakshināmūrti, may this obeisance be!

To him who like a magician or even like a great yogi displays, by his own power, this universe which at the beginning is undifferentiated like the sprout in the seed, but which is made differentiated under the varied conditions of space, time, and *karma* and posited by *māyā* to him, the Guru Dakshināmūrti, may this obeisance be!

To him whose luminosity alone, which is of the nature of existence, shines forth, entering the objective world which is like the non-existent; to him who instructs those who resort to him through the text 'That thou art': to him by realizing whom there will be no more falling into the ocean of birth; to him who is the refuge of the ascetics, the Guru Dakshināmūrti, may this obeisance be!

To him who is luminous like the light of a lamp set in a pot with many holes: to him whose knowledge moves outward through the eye and other sense organs: to him who is effulgent as 'I know', and the entire universe shines after him: to him, the unmoving Guru Dakshināmūrti, may this obeisance be!

They who know the 'I' as body, breath, senses, intellect, or the void, are deluded like women and children, and the blind and the stupid, and talk much. To him who destroys the great delusion produced by ignorance: to him who removes the obstacles to knowledge, the Guru Dakshināmūrti, may this obeisance be!

To him, who sleeps when the manifested mind gets resolved, on account of the veiling by *māyā*, like the sun or the moon in eclipse, and on waking recognizes self-existence in the form 'I have slept till now': to him the Guru of all that moves and moves not, Dakshināmūrti, may this obeisance be!

To him who, by means of the hand-pose indicating illumination, manifests to his devotees his own Self that forever shines within as 'I', constantly, in all the inconstant states such as infancy, etc, and waking, etc – to him whose eye is of the form of the fire of knowledge, the Guru Dakshināmūrti, may this obeisance be!

To the self who, deluded by *māyā*, sees, in dreaming and waking, the universe in its distinctions such as cause and effect, master and servant, disciple and teacher, and father and son, to him, the Guru of the world, Dakshināmūrti, may this obeisance be!

To him whose eightfold form is all this moving and unmoving universe, appearing as earth, water, fire, air, ether, the sun, the moon, and soul: beyond whom, supreme and all-pervading, there exists naught else for those who enquire – to him the gracious Guru Dakshinamurti, may this obeisance be!

Since, in this hymn, the all-self-hood has thus been explained, by listening to it, by reflecting on its meaning, by meditating on it, and by reciting it, there will come about lordship together with the supreme splendour consisting in all-self-hood; thence will be achieved, again, the unimpeded supernormal power presenting itself in eight forms.

GURUSTUTI

Introduction by
Sri Bhagavan Ramana Maharshi

When Shankaracharya was going about the country debating with the exponents of the various schools of thought and overcoming them, he once came to the town of Mahishmati in the north, where Mandana Mishra the exponent of Vedic rituals lived. He overcame him in debate but his wife refused to concede victory until she was also defeated. So, Shankaracharya argued with her and defeated her in all subjects except erotica. He then asked for a respite of one month and after shedding his body in a cave under the custody of his disciples, entered into the dead body of King Amaruka and sported among the hundred queens in the guise of their husband. When the disciples found that the period specified by their Guru had already expired they grew anxious. So some of them went to him in the disguise of minstrels and sang the following hymn (to remind him).

Text

1. That is the Truth which the wise realize as the Self, the residuum left over on withdrawing from external objects, with or without form (ether, air, fire, water and earth), by a careful application of the scriptural text 'Not this, not this'. That thou art!
2. That is the Truth which, after generating the fundamentals (ether, air, fire, water, and earth), and entering the world, lies hidden beneath the five sheaths, and which has been threshed out

by the wise with the pestle of discernment, just as the grain is recovered by threshing and winnowing the chaff. That thou art!

3. Just as wild horses are broken-in by whipping and stabling them, so also the unruly senses, straying among objects, are lashed by the whip of discrimination, showing that objects are unreal, and are tethered by the rope of pure intellect to the Self by the wise. Such is the Truth. That thou art!

4. The Truth has been ascertained by the wise to be the substratum which is different from the waking, dream, and deep sleep states, its own expanded modes, which indeed are held together by it like the flowers strung together on a garland. That thou art!

5. That is the Truth which the scriptures show to be the primal cause of all, elucidating the point clearly by such texts as '*Purusha* is all this', 'like gold in ornaments of gold', etc. That thou art!

6. The Truth has been forcefully proclaimed by the scriptures in such texts as 'He who is in the sun, is in man.' 'He who shines in the sun, shines in the right eye,' etc. That thou art!

7. What pure Brahmins seek so eagerly by repetition of the Vedas, by religious gifts, by earnest application of their hard-earned knowledge, and by renunciation, is the Truth. That thou art!

8. That is the Truth which the valiant have got by seeking, with controlled mind, with abstinence, penance, etc, and by diving into the Self by the self. Realizing it, they are considered to be heroes with their highest purpose accomplished. That is the transcendental *Satchidananda* (Being-Consciousness-Bliss) after gaining which there is nothing more to worry about since perfect peace reigns. That thou art!

On hearing these (verses) the Acharya bade them (his disciples) go away and promptly came out of the body of the King and re-entered his own. He then went to the lady (wife of Mandana Mishra) and, after defeating her, made the two of them (she and her husband) his followers. Thereafter he went on his way enlightening the whole world.

Hastamalaka Stotra

Introduction by
Sri Bhagavan Ramana Maharshi

When Sankara, the Guru of the world, was travelling in the western parts of India and overcoming (in debate) the expounders of the various schools of thought, he once came to a village known as Srīvali. When a Brahmin inhabitant of the village named Prabhākara heard about his arrival he went to him with his thirteen-year-old son. He prostrated before Sankara and made his son also prostrate. He then explained that the boy had been dumb from his childhood, that he had no likes and dislikes, nor a sense of honour and dishonour, and that he was completely inactive. The Guru then raised the boy up and asked him as follows in a cheerful tone.

Text

1. 'Who are you? Whose child are you? Whither are you bound? What is your name? Whence you have come? Oh Child! I should like to hear your reply to these questions.' Thus spoke Sri Shankaracharya to the boy, and Hastamalaka replied as follows.
2. I am neither man, God, *yaksha*, brahmin, kshatriya, vaisya, sudra, *brahmachāri*, householder, forest-dweller, nor *sannyāsi*; but I am pure awareness alone.
3. Just as the sun causes all worldly movements, so do I — the

ever-present, conscious Self — cause the mind to be active and the senses to function. Again, just as the ether is all-pervading yet devoid of any specific qualities, so am I free from all qualities.

4. I am the conscious Self, ever-present and associated with everything in the same manner as heat is always associated with fire. I am that eternal, undifferentiated, unshaken Consciousness, on account of which the insentient mind and senses function, each in its own manner.

5. I am that conscious Self of whom the ego is not independent as the image in a mirror is not independent of the object reflected.

6. I am the unqualified, conscious Self, existing even after the extinction of *buddhi* just as the object remains ever the same even after the removal of the reflecting mirror.

7. I am eternal Consciousness, dissociated from the mind and senses. I am the mind of the mind, the eye of the eye, ear of the ear and so on. I am not cognizable by the mind and senses.

8. I am the eternal, single, conscious Self, reflected in various intellects, just as the sun is reflected on the surface of various sheets of water.

9. I am the single, conscious Self illumining all intellects, just as the sun simultaneously illumines all eyes so that they perceive objects.

10. Only those eyes that are helped by the sun are capable of seeing objects, not others. The source from which the sun derives its power is myself.

11. Just as the reflection of the sun on agitated waters seems to break up, but remains perfect on a calm surface, so also am I, the conscious Self, unrecognizable in agitated intellects though I clearly shine in those which are calm.

12. Just as a fool thinks that the sun is entirely lost when it is

hidden by dense clouds, so do people think that the ever-free Self is bound.

13. Just as the ether is all-pervading and unaffected by contact, so also does the ever-conscious Self pervade everything without being affected in any way. I am that Self.

14. Just as a transparent crystal takes on the lines of its background, but is in no way changed thereby, and just as the unchanging moon on being reflected on undulating surfaces appears agitated, so is it with You, the all-pervading God.

The father of the boy was speechless with wonder at those words. But the Acharya said to him: 'He has become your son because of his incomplete austerities. This is your good fortune. He will not be of any use to you in this world. Let him stay with me.' He bade him go back and, taking the boy with him, proceeded on his way. The disciples then asked him: "How did this boy attain the state of *Brahman* without hearing, etc?' The Guru replied: 'His mother left her two-year-old child in the care of a great and highly accomplished *yogi* who was practising austerities on the bank of the Yamuna while she went to bathe in the river with some women. The child toddled towards the water and was drowned. Out of his compassion for the disconsolate mother the sadhu forsook his body and entered that of the child. That is why this boy has attained this high state.'

ĀTMA BŌDHA

(Knowledge of the Self)

A Muslim devotee once sent a Tamil translation of this Sanskrit poem of Shankaracharya to Bhagavan. Bhagavan prepared the following new translation in Tamil. He completed the whole work in one night!

'Can Shankara, the enlightener of the Self, be different from one's own Self? Who but he, does this day, abiding as the inmost Self in me, speak this in the Tamil language?'

- Sri Bhagavan

1. This - *Ātma Bōdha* – is meant to fulfil the want of the seekers of liberation who, by their prolonged *tapas*, have already cleansed themselves of impurities and become mentally peaceful and free from desires.

2. Of all the means to liberation, knowledge is the only direct one – as essential as fire to cooking; without it, liberation cannot be gained.

3. Not being opposed to ignorance, *karma* does not destroy it. On the other hand, knowledge destroys ignorance as surely as light does darkness.

4. Owing to ignorance, the Self now appears to be covered up; on the removal of ignorance, the pure Self will shine forth of Itself, like the sun after the dispersal of clouds.

5. The *jīva* is mixed up with ignorance. By constant practice of knowledge the *jīva* become pure, because knowledge

disappears (along with ignorance), as the cleansing nut with the impurities in the water.

But here is the world; how can the Self alone be real and non-dual?

6. *Samsāra* is full of likes and dislikes and other opposites. Like a dream, it seems real for the time being; but, on waking, it vanishes because it is unreal.

    Because the dream is negated on waking, I know it to be unreal; but the world persists and I find it only real.

7. So long as the substratum of all, the non-dual *Brahman* is not seen, the world seems real — like illusory silver in a piece of mother-of-pearl.

    But the world is so diverse; yet, you say there is one only.

8. Like bubbles rising on the surface of the waters of the ocean, all the worlds arise from, stay in and resolve into the Supreme Being (*Paramēsa*) who is the root cause and prop of all.

9. In the Being-Consciousness-Bliss, which is all permeating, eternal Vishnu, all these diverse objects and individuals appear (as phenomena) like various ornaments made of gold.

    Yes, but what about the numberless individual souls?

10. Just as the all-pervading *ākāsa* (ether) appears fragmented in different objects (as in a pit, a jar, a house, a theatre hall, etc) but remains undifferentiated on the limitations falling away, similarly with the single, non-dual ruler of the senses (seeming to function as gods, men, cattle, etc).

    But the individuals have different traits and function according to different conditions.

11. The traits etc are also superimposed. Pure water (tasteless by itself) tastes sweet, bitter, salty etc, according to the admixture in it (*upādhis*). Similarly, race, name, status, etc, are all superimposed on the non-dual Self of all. What are these *upādhis* which play such tricks on the Self? They are

gross, subtle and very subtle as described here.

12. The gross body made up of the five gross elements (earth, water, fire, air and ether) is meant to reap the fruits of past actions in the shape of pleasure and pain.

13. The subtle body consisting of the five airs, the mind, intellect, the ten senses and made up of subtle elements is also meant for enjoyment (as in dreams).

14. Inexpressible and beginningless ignorance is said to be the causal body (as in deep sleep). Know the Self to be other than these three *upādhis*.

    Doubt: *If so, why is the Self not evident to me? On the other hand,* Sruti *says, 'This* Purusha *is made up of* annarasa *(essence of food).'*

15. Just as a clear crystal (itself colourless) appears red, blue, yellow, etc, according to the background, so also the Self, pure and untainted, seems to be identical with the body, the senses, the mind, intellect or blissful ignorance (*pancha kosas*) when in contact with them.

16. Just as husking the paddy exposes the grain within (the rice), so also should one judiciously separate the pure *ātman* from the sheaths covering it.

    Ātman is said to be everywhere. Why should it then be judiciously looked for within the five sheaths?

17. Though always and everywhere present, the Self does not shine forth in all places. Just as light is reflected only in a transparent medium, so also the Self is clearly seen in the intellect only.

18. The Self is realized in the intellect as the witness of the activities of, and yet separate from the body, the senses, the mind, intellect and gross nature (*prakriti*) as is a king in relation to his subjects.

    The Self seems to participate in their activities; so he cannot be different from them, nor be their witness.

19. Just as the moon seems to move when the clouds around her

move, so also the Self seems to the undiscriminating to be active, when actually, the senses are active.

To be active, the body etc must also be intelligent; they are said to be inert. How can they act without the intelligent Self participating in their actions?

20. Just as men do their duties in the light of the sun (but the sun does not participate in them), so also the body, senses, etc, function in the light of the Self without its participating in them.

True, the Self alone is intelligence. I know myself to be born, growing, decaying, happy, or unhappy and so on. Am I right?

21. No. The characteristics (birth, death, etc) of the body and the senses are superimposed on the Being-Consciousness-Bliss as is the blue in the sky by those who do not discriminate.

22. So also the characteristics of the mind, such as agency, etc, are by ignorance superimposed on the *ātman*, as are the movements of water on the moon reflected in it.

23. Only when the intellect is manifested, likes and dislikes, pleasure and pain are felt. In deep sleep, the intellect remaining latent, they are not felt. Therefore, they are of the intellect and not of the *ātman* (the Self). Here is the real nature of the *ātman*.

24. As light is the very sun, coldness the water, heat the fire, so also the eternal, pure Being-Consciousness-Bliss is the very Self.

At some time or other, every individual experiences, 'I am happy', and thus Being-Consciousness-Bliss experience is plain. How can one make the experience permanent and unchanging?

25. Being-Consciousness is of the Self; the 'I' mode or modification is of the intellect; these are distinctly two. However, owing to ignorance, the individual mixes them together and thinks 'I know' and acts accordingly.

26. Never is there any change (or action) in *ātman* nor

knowledge in the intellect. Only the *jīva* is deluded into thinking itself to be the knower, doer and seer.

27. Like the snake in the rope, mistaking the *jīva* for the Self, one is subject to fear. If, on the other hand, one knows oneself not as a *jīva* but as the supreme Self, one is altogether free from fear.

28. Only the Self illumines the senses, intellect, etc, as a lamp does objects such as pots. The Self is not illumined by them as they are inert.

     If the Self cannot be made known by the intellect, there will be no knower to know the Self and the Self cannot be known.

29. To see a light, no other light is needed. So also, the Self being self-effulgent, needs no other means of knowledge. It shines of itself.

     If so, everyone must be self-realized, effortlessly, but it is not so.

30. On the strength of the Vedic teaching, 'Not this, not this', eliminate all the adjuncts (*upādhis*) and with the help of the *mahāvakyas*, realize the identity of the *jīvatman* (individual self) with the *paramātman* (the supreme Self).

31. The whole objective world such as the body, is born of ignorance and transient like a bubble on water. Know the Self to be distinct from it and identical with *Brahman* (the Supreme).

32. Being distinct from the gross body, birth, death, old age, debility, etc, do not pertain to me. Not being the senses, I have no connection with the objects of the senses such as sound etc.

33. The *srutis* declare: 'I am not the vital air (*prāna*) — not the mind, (but) (pure Being).' Not being the mind I am free from likes and dislikes, fear etc.

34. 'I am free from qualities and actionless, eternal, undifferentiated, untainted, unchanging, formless, ever free and pure.'

35. 'Like ether, I am always pervading all, in and out, unswerving,

ever equal in all, pure, untainted, clear and unshaken.'

36. 'That which remains eternal, pure, ever-free, all alone, unbroken bliss, non-dual, Being-Consciousness-Bliss, transcendent *Brahman* (the same) am I.'

37. Long, constant practice of 'I am *Brahman* only' destroys all *vāsanās* (latent tendencies), born of ignorance as an efficacious remedy (*rasāyana*) eradicates a disease.

38. Be dispassionate, keep the senses under control; and let the mind not wander; sit in a solitary place and meditate on the Self as infinite and one alone.

39. Keep the mind pure; with keen intellect, resolve all that is objective into the Self and always meditate on the Self as clear and single like ether.

40. Having discarded all names and forms, you are now the knower of the Supreme Being and will remain as perfect Consciousness-Bliss.

41. Being the same as Consciousness-Bliss, there is no longer any differentiation such as the knower and the known; and the Self shines forth as Itself.'

42. If in this manner by process of constant meditation, the two pieces of wood, namely the Self and the ego are rubbed together, the flames from the fire of knowledge burn away the whole range of ignorance.

43. On knowledge destroying ignorance in this way, like the light of dawn scattering the darkness of night, the Self will rise like the sun in all its glory.

44. True – the Self is always here and now; yet it is not apparent, owing to ignorance. On ignorance being destroyed the Self seems as if it were gained, like the necklace on one's own neck.[1]

45. Just as in darkness a post is mistaken for a thief, so is *Brahman* in ignorance mistaken for a *jīva*. If, however, the true nature of a *jīva* is seen, delusion vanishes.

46. Knowledge arising on the experience of reality immediately destroys the ignorant perception of 'I' and 'mine', which resemble the delusion of direction in darkness.

47. A *jnāni* who is a perfectly self-realized *yogi*, sees by the eye of wisdom all objective phenomena to be in and of the Self and thus the Self to be the sole being.

    How does he then act in the world?

48. Just as clay is the only material from which different utensils are formed (such as pots, jars, etc), so he sees that the Self, too, is the whole universe and there is nothing but the Self.

49. In order to be liberated while yet alive, the sage should completely eschew the adjuncts (*upādhis*), and thus gain the real nature of Being-Consciousness-Bliss, like the maggot that turns into a wasp.

50. Having crossed the ocean of illusion and having killed the demons of likes and dislikes, the *yogi*, now united to *shānti* (peace), finds delight in the Self and so remains in his own glory.

51. The *jīvanmukta*, freed from all desire for transient, external pleasures, delights in his own Self and remains clear and steady like lamp in a pot.

52. Like the *ākāsa* (ether) which remains untainted by the objects contained therein, the *muni* (sage) remains untainted by the adjuncts (*upādhis*) covering him. Being the all-knower he remains like one that knows not, and moves about like the air uncontaminated by the objects it touches.

53. On the dissolution of the adjuncts (the body, senses, etc), the sage now freed from particularities merges in the all permeating Being (Vishnu), like water in water, ether in ether or fire in fire.

54. There is no gain over and above this gain, no pleasure over and above this bliss, no knowledge over and above this knowledge, know this to be *Brahman*.

55. That on seeing which nothing remains to see, on becoming which there is no more return to *samsāra*, on knowing which nothing remains to know, know that to be *Brahman*.

56. What fills everything, above, below and around, itself Being-Consciousness-Bliss, non-dual, infinite, eternal, one only, know that to be *Brahman*.

57. What remains as immutable, unbroken Bliss, and as one only, that which even the scriptures indirectly denote by the process of elimination as 'not this, not this', know the same to be *Brahman*.

58. Dependent on a fraction of the inexhaustible Bliss of the *ātman*, all the gods such as Brahma enjoy bliss according to their grades.

59. Like the butter in milk, the objective universe is contained in it; all the activities are based on it alone. Therefore *Brahman* is all-pervading.

60. What is neither subtle nor gross, short nor long, produced nor spent, what is devoid of form, attribute, caste, and name, know it to be *Brahman*.

61. By whose light the sun and other luminaries shine forth, but which is not itself illumined by them, and in whose light all this is seen, know it to be *Brahman*.

62. Like fire in a piece of red-hot iron, *Brahman* permeates the whole world in and out and all through, makes it shine and itself also shines by itself.

63. *Brahman* is distinct from the universe, yet there remains nothing apart from *Brahman*. Should any other than *Brahman* appear, it is only an illusion like water in a mirage.

64. Whatever is seen or heard, it cannot be different from *Brahman*. True knowledge finds *Brahman* to be Being-Consciousness-Bliss and one without a second.

65. Only the eye of wisdom can see the omnipresent Being-Consciousness-Bliss, but not the eye of ignorance for a

blind eye cannot see the sun.

66. Like gold freed from dross, the *jīva* (*sādhaka*) has all his impurities burnt away by the fire of knowledge bursting into flames fanned by *sravana*, *manana* and *nidhidhyāsana* (hearing, reflection and contemplation) and now he shines forth by himself.

67. Because the sun of knowledge, the chaser of darkness has risen the *ātman* shines in the expanse of the Heart as the omnipresent sustainer of all and illumines all.

68. He who bathes in the clear, warm, ever-refreshing water of the *ātman*, which being available everywhere, here and now, need not be sought for in special centres and seasons, such a one remains actionless. He is the knower of all; he pervades all and is ever immortal.

Drik Drisya Vivēka

Translated into Tamil and with an introductory verse by Sri Bhagavan Ramana Maharshi

Oh thou divine Shankara,
Thou art the Subject,
That has knowledge
Of subject and object.
Let the subject in me be destroyed
As subject and object.
For thus in my mind arises
The light as the single Siva.

Introduction

Written by Sri Bhagavan to His translation in Tamil of Sri Shankaracharya's Drik Drisya Vivēka:

'*Brahman* is only one and non-dual' declare the *Srutis*. Since *Brahman* is the sole reality, according to *advaita*, how is it that *Brahman* is not apparent to us, whereas the *prapancha* (world, i.e. non-*Brahman*) is so vivid? Thus questions the advanced *sādhaka*.

In one's own Self, which is not other than *Brahman*, there is a mysterious power known as *avidyā* (ignorance) which is beginningless and not separate from the Self. Its characteristics are veiling, and presentation of diversity. Just as the pictures in a cinema, though not visible either in sunlight or in darkness, become visible in a spot of light in the midst of darkness, so in the darkness of ignorance there appears the reflected light of the Self, illusory and scattered taking the form of thought. This is the primal thought known as the ego, *jīva* or *karta* (doer), having the mind as the medium of its perceptions. The mind has a store of latent tendencies which it projects as the object of a shadow-show in the waking and dream states. This show, however, is mistaken for real by the *jīva*. The veiling aspect of the mind first hides the real nature of the Self and then presents the objective world to view. Just as the waters of the ocean do not seem different from the waves, so also for the duration of objective phenomena, the Self, though itself the sole being, is made to appear not different from them. Turn away from the delusion caused by the latent tendencies and false notions of interior and exterior. By such constant practice of *sahaja samādhi*, the veiling power vanishes and the non-dual Self is left over to shine forth as *Brahman* itself. This is the whole secret of the *advaita* doctrine as taught by the master to the advanced *sādhaka*. Here the same teaching is contained, which Sri Shankarācharya has expounded concisely without any elaboration, in the following text.

The Text

All our perception pertains to the non-Self. The immutable Seer is indeed the Self. All the countless scriptures proclaim only discrimination between Self and non-Self.

The world we see, being seen by the eye, is *drisya* (object); the eye which sees it is *drik* (subject). But the eye, being perceived by the mind is *drisya* (object) and the mind which sees it is *drik* (subject). The mind, with its thoughts perceived by the Self, is *drisya* (object) and the Self is *drik* (subject). The Self cannot be *drisya* (object), not being perceived by anything else. The forms perceived are various, blue and yellow, gross and subtle, tall and short, and so on; but the eye that sees them remains one and the same. Similarly, the varying qualities of the eye, such as blindness, dullness and keenness and of the ears and other organs, are perceived by the mind singly. So, too, the various characteristics of the mind, such as desire, determination, doubt, faith, want of faith, courage, want of courage, fear, shyness, discrimination, good and bad, are all perceived by the Self singly. The Self neither rises nor sets, neither increases nor decays. It shines of its own luminosity. It illumines everything else without the need for aid from other sources.

Buddhi, as the sum total of the inner organs, in contact with the reflected consciousness has two aspects. One is called egoity and the other mind. This contact of the *buddhi* with the reflected consciousness is like the identity of a red-hot iron ball with fire. Hence the gross body passes for a conscious entity. The contact establishing identity between the ego and the reflected Consciousness, is of three kinds.

1. The identification of the ego with the reflected Consciousness is natural or innate.
2. The identification of the ego with the body is due to past *karma*.
3. The identification of the ego with the witness is due to ignorance.

The natural or innate contact continues as long as the *buddhi*, but on realization of the Self it proves to be false. The third-mentioned contact is broken when it is discovered by experience that there is no sort of contact of anything at all with the Self, which is Being. The second-mentioned contact, that born of past *karma*, ceases to exist on the destruction of innate tendencies (*vāsanās*). In the deep sleep state, when the body is inert, the ego is fully merged (in the causal ignorance). The ego is half manifest in the dream state, and its being fully manifest is the waking state. It is the mode or modification of thought (with its latent tendencies) that creates the inner world of dreams in the dream state and the outer world in the waking state. The subtle body, which is the material cause of mind and ego, experiences the three states and also birth and death.

Māyā of the causal body has its powers of projecting (*rajas*) and veiling (*tamas*). It is the projecting power that creates everything from the subtle body to the gross universe of names and forms. These are produced in the *Sat-Chit-Ananda* (Being-Consciousness-Bliss) like foam in the ocean. The veiling power operates in such a way that internally the distinction between subject and object cannot be perceived, and externally that between *Brahman* and the phenomenal world. This indeed is the cause of *samsāra*. The individual with his reflected light of Consciousness is the subtle body existing in close proximity with the Self that is *vyavahārika* (the empirical Self). This individual character of the empirical Self appears in the witness or *sākshin* also through false superimposition. But on the extinction of the veiling power (*tamas*), the distinction between witness and the empirical Self becomes clear; and the superimposition also drops away. Similarly, *Brahman* shines as the phenomenal world of names and forms only through the effect of the veiling power which conceals the distinction between them. When the veiling ends, the distinction between the two is perceived, for none of the activities of the phenomenal world exist in *Brahman*.

Of the five characteristics, Being, Consciousness, Bliss, name and form, the first three pertain to *Brahman* and name and form to the world. The three aspects of Being, Consciousness and Bliss exist equally in the five elements of ether, air, fire, water and earth and in devas (gods), animals, men, etc, whereas the names and forms are different. Therefore, be indifferent to names and forms, concentrate on Being-Consciousness-Bliss and constantly practice *samādhi* (identity with *Brahman*) within the heart or outside.

This practice of *samādhi* (identity with *Brahman*) is of two kinds; *savikalpa* (in which the distinction between knower, knowledge and known is not lost) and *nirvikalpa* (in which the above distinction is lost). *Savikalpa samādhi* again is of two kinds: that which is associated with words (sound), and meditation on one's own consciousness as the witness of thought forms such as desire, which is *savikalpa samādhi* (internal), associated with (cognizable) objects. Realizing one's Self as 'I am Being-Consciousness-Bliss without duality, unattached, self-effulgent', is *savikalpa samādhi* (internal) associated with words (sound). Giving up both objects and sound forms of the aforesaid two modes of *samādhi* and being completely absorbed in the Bliss experienced by the realization of the Self is *nirvikalpa samādhi* (internal). In this state steady abidance is obtained, like the unflickering flame of a light kept in a place free from wind. So also, in the heart, becoming indifferent to external objects of name and form and perceiving only Being of (or as) *Sat*, is *savikalpa samādhi* (external) associated with objects; and being aware continually of that *Sat* (true existence) as the unbroken single essence of *Brahman* is *savikalpa samādhi* (external) associated with words (sound). After these two experiences, Being, which is uninterrupted like the waveless ocean, is *nirvikalpa samādhi* (external). One who meditates should spend his time perpetually in these six kinds of *samādhi*. By these, the attachment to the body is destroyed and the mind that perpetually abides in the Supreme Self (*paramātman*) wherever it may wander, is everywhere spontaneously in *samādhi*. By this constant practice of *samādhi*, the supreme Self, who is both highest and lowliest, who encompasses *paramātman* as well as *jīvatman* is directly experienced, and then the knot of the heart is loosened; all doubts are destroyed and all *karma*s (activities) cease too.

Of the three modes of individual being, the limited self (as in deep sleep), the empirical self (as in the waking state) and the

dreaming self, only the individual limited by the deep sleep state
is the true Self (*paramārthika*). Even he is but an idea. The
Absolute alone is the true Self. In reality and by nature he is
Brahman itself, only superimposition creates the limitations of
individuality in the Absolute. It is to the *paramārthika jīva* that the
identity of *Tat Twam Asi* (That thou Art) and other great texts of
the Upanishads applies, and not to any other. The great *māyā* (the
superimposition without beginning) with her veiling and
projecting power (*tamas* and *rajas*) veils the single indivisible
Brahman and, in that *Brahman*, creates the world and individuals.
The individual (*jīva*), a concept of the empirical self in the *buddhi*,
is indeed the actor and enjoyer and the entire phenomenal world
is its object of enjoyment. From time without beginning, till the
attainment of liberation, individual and world have an empirical
existence. They are both empirical. The empirical individual
appears to have the power of sleep in the shape of the veiling and
projecting powers. It is associated with Consciousness. The
power covers first the individual empirical self and the cognized
universe, and then these are imagined in dream. These dream
perceptions and the individual who perceives them are illusory,
because they exist only during the period of dream experience. We
affirm their illusory nature, because on waking up from dream no
one sees the dream, no one sees the dream objects. The dreaming
self experiences the dream world as real, while the empirical self
experiences the empirical world as real but, when the *paramārthika
jīva* is realized, knows it to be unreal. The *paramārthika jīva*, as
distinguished from those of the waking and dream experiences, is
identical with *Brahman*. He has no 'other'. If he does see any
'other', he knows it to be illusory.

The sweetness, liquidity, and coldness of water are characteristics present equally in waves and foam. So, too, the Being-
Consciousness-Bliss character of the Self (the *paramārthika*) is
present in the empirical self and through him in the dream self

also, because of their being only illusory creations in the Self. The foam with its qualities, such as coldness, subsides in the waves, the waves with their characteristics, such as liquidity, subside in the water, and the ocean alone exists as at first. Similarly, the dream self and its objects are absorbed in the empirical self; then the empirical world with its characteristics is absorbed in the *paramārthika* and, as at first, Being-Consciousness-Bliss which is *Brahman* shines alone.

Vichāra Mani Mālā

(Jewel Garland of Enquiry)

This is a compilation of the salient points extracted by Bhagavan Sri Ramana Maharshi from a large volume in Tamil known as Vichāra Sāgara *(Ocean of Enquiry), which itself was a translation from the original in Hindi by Mahātma Nischaldas. On being appealed to by a devotee, Arunāchala Mudaliar, who complained that the volume in Tamil was too difficult to read and understand, Sri Bhagavan graciously made the following extracts.*

Invocation

I am that *Brahman* which is bliss, which is eternal, effulgent, all-pervasive, the substratum of names and forms, which is not cognized by the impure intellect, but is cognized by the pure intellect, stainless and boundless. That is to say, when one discards the *jīva* (individual being) of the form of *ahamkāra* (ego-sense), which is the apparent meaning of the word 'I', what remains merely as the effulgent and conscious *ātman* (Self), which is the implied meaning of the word 'I', is *Brahman*. This can also be understood from the following words of Arunagiriar's experience: 'After swallowing me who had the form of "I" (ego), that supreme Being remained as mere Self.'

The Text

The noble aspirant for liberation whose mind has become pure and one-pointed by the cessation of evil thoughts, as a result of the motiveless acts and meditations performed by him in his former lives, and who is subject only to the defect of the concealing power (*āvarana shakti*) in the form of ignorance of the Self, and who possesses the four qualifications of discrimination, dispassion, the six virtues like self-control and yearning for liberation, being unable to endure the miseries of *samsāra*, approaches the Sadguru who is compassionate, who has realized the meaning of *Vēdānta* and who is established in *Brahman*, and, after prostrating before him with fear and reverence, questions him thus.

Disciple: Swami, what are the means of putting an end to the miseries of *samsāra* like birth and death and of attaining supreme bliss?

Guru: Oh Disciple! What a delusion! You are always of the nature of bliss. There is not the least trace of the miseries of *samsāra* in you. Therefore do not take upon yourself the miseries of birth, etc. You are the conscious *Brahman* which is free from birth and death.

Disciple: Is not liberation the cessation of misery and the attainment of supreme bliss? If I am (already) of the nature of bliss how is it possible for me to attain the bliss which is always attained and similarly to get rid of the misery which never existed?

Guru: This is possible just as one can seek and find a bracelet which was on one's arm all the time but which one had forgotten about, and on finding it look upon it as a new acquisition. It is possible as in the case of the serpent which, at no time present in the rope, was mistaken for one, but which seemed to be there and seems to disappear when one discovers that it is only a piece of rope.

Disciple: Will the non-existence of misery and the existence of bliss co-exist in one and the same state (*lit.* substance) of liberation?

Guru: They will. Just as the non-existence of the imagined serpent is the existence of the rope, the non-existence of the imagined misery is the existence of bliss.

Disciple: As bliss arises only from contact with objects, how can I be said to be (of the nature of) bliss?

Guru: The bliss of the Self will not be felt in the intellect which is distracted by desires for objects by one who does not know the Self. When the object of desire is obtained the intellect becomes steady for a moment and turns inward. Then the bliss of the Self is reflected in it and this gives rise to a delusion that there was bliss in the object. But when other objects are desired this bliss vanishes. It is similar to the bliss which one experiences on the arrival of one's son from a foreign country. It does not last as long as the object which seemed to be the cause of it. Further, bliss is experienced in the state of *samādhi* and deep sleep, even without objects. Therefore there is no bliss in objects. The Self alone is bliss. It is because the bliss of the Self alone is experienced by all, that all are proclaimed by the Vedas to be of the form of bliss.

Disciple: But does the sage (*jnāni*) who knows the Self desire objects and experience bliss, or does he not?

Guru: Although he may desire objects and experience bliss like the ignorant person, he does not imagine that bliss to be any different from the bliss of the Self.

Disciple: When the misery of birth, death, etc, is actually experienced how can it be said that it never exists in me?

Guru: Know that the world of birth, death, etc, is an illusory appearance like the serpent in the rope and blueness in the sky, or like dreams, due to your ignorance of your Self which is *Brahman*.

Disciple: What is the support (*ādhāra*) for this extensive world?

Guru: Just as the rope is the support and basis for the delusive serpent which appears when the rope is not recognized as such, so you are the support and basis for the world which appears when you do not know your Self.

Disciple: Kindly explain distinctly the ideas of support (*ādhāra*) and basis (*adhishtāna*).

Guru: Even in the unreal serpent there is a concept 'this' which is mixed up with the general concept 'this' underlying the rope. Similarly in the unreal world there is a concept 'it exists' which is mixed up with the general concept of existence underlying the Self. This existence is the support of the world. Again, just as there is the particular concept 'rope' (besides the general concept of 'this') there is also the particular concept of the Self, namely that it is unattached, immutable, ever-liberated, all-pervasive, etc. This is not cognized at the time of the delusion, but, when cognized, removes the delusion. This particular concept of Self is the basis of the world.

Disciple: Corresponding to the seer who is separate from the rope which is the support and basis of the serpent, who is the seer apart from me who is the support and basis of the world?

Guru: If the basis is insentient a separate seer is necessary. If the basis is sentient it will itself be the seer. Just as the witnessing consciousness which is the basis of the dream is itself the seer of the dream, you are yourself the seer of the world.

Disciple: If the world of the waking state comes into existence and falsely appears like dreams through nescience, why should we speak of any distinction between the waking state and the dream state and say that the waking state has relative (empirical: *vyavahārika*) reality while the dream state has only personal (*pratibhāsika*) reality?

Guru: Since a dream appears without the help of the appropriate time, space and materials on account of nescience accompanied by the defect (*dosham*) of sleep, it is spoken of as a personal state. Since the waking state appears in the supreme Self which is free from time, space and materials, owing to nescience alone, it is spoken of as the relative state. They are thus described with reference to the three states of reality (personal, relative and absolute).

When we think clearly there is no difference between them. Nor is there any difference between the waking and the dream state. Undifferentiated consciousness is the only true reality. Whatever is different from it is personal and has nescience as its material cause and consciousness as its basis.

Disciple: If that is so why is there a cessation of the dream state even in the absence of knowledge of *Brahman* while the state of waking does not cease without knowledge of *Brahman*?

Guru: Although there cannot be complete cessation of the dream state until there is knowledge of *Brahman* in the waking state, the defect of sleep, which is the immediate cause of the dream, may disappear by the emergence of the waking state which is inimical to it.

Disciple: The object of the waking state prior to the dream exist in the waking state succeeding the dream also. But the objects of one dream are not seen in the next dream. How then can the two states be regarded as similar?

Guru: All objects are the transformation by nescience of the underlying consciousness. When a concept arises they also arise and when a concept ceases they also cease. Therefore it cannot be said that the objects of the previous waking state exist in the subsequent waking state also. As in a dream they (the objects of the subsequent waking state) come into existence for the time being. Therefore both are similar.

Disciple: Since a man who wakes up from a dream believes the objects he sees to be the same as before his dream, it cannot be said that they come into existence only when there is knowledge of them. Objects exist permanently prior to and after the knowledge of them.

Guru: Just as the things which come into existence for the time being in a dream seem to have existed unchanged for a long time, so also do the objects which come in existence in the waking state on account of strong nescience. The ideas of cause and effect in respect of these objects are also similar.

Disciple: If the bondage of *samsāra* came into existence on account of ignorance of the Self, when did that ignorance arise?

Guru: The ignorance, arising from the Self, which is *Brahman*, is mere imagination (*kalpita*) and has no beginning.

Disciple: Since darkness cannot exist in the sun, how can nescience exist in *Brahman* which is pure consciousness? Even if it exists, it cannot exist in what is clearly known or in what is not at all known. Superimposition of a false reality upon a true, is possible only when the general aspect of something is known and not its particular aspect. *Brahman* has no parts like general and particular; it is attributeless; so how can there be the super-imposition of bondage?

Guru: Although *Brahman* is consciousness, the general (indistinct) aspect of that all-pervasive consciousness which is of the nature of effulgence is not inimical to nescience, but helpful to it. In deep sleep nescience co-exists with the Consciousness of the Self. The general (possibility of) fire within the wood is not inimical to darkness, but helpful to it. But as the actualized (manifest) fire produced by rubbing the wood is inimical to darkness, so also the distinct consciousness produced in the mind as *Brahman* is inimical to nescience. Although *Brahman* is without attributes (and cannot therefore be cognized) its general existence is known even in the state of nescience in the form of 'I am', while its particular aspects like consciousness, bliss, etc, are not then known, but are known only in the state of knowledge. As appearances are the result of nescience, there can be the bondage of superimposition in the attributeless *Brahman*, which is known as existence and unknown as consciousness and bliss.

Disciple: Although the world is unreal it is the cause of miseries like birth and death. An unreal nightmare will not occur if *japa* is done (before going to sleep). Analogous to this, what can be done to prevent the appearance of the world?

Guru: That which appears owing to ignorance of something will cease to appear only through knowledge of that something. The serpent and the silver which appear on account of the ignorance of the rope and the nacre will disappear only through knowledge of them. Similarly the world which appears on account of ignorance of the Self will disappear only through knowledge of the Self. *Brahman* is infinite, homogeneous, unattached to anything, without birth, etc, invisible and without name and form. The nescience imagined in it and its effects, namely the individual, the Lord and the world, are unreal in all the three periods of time. Whatever is seen is the play of the intellect which is the effect of that nescience. *Brahman*, while remaining unmoved, illumines the intellect. This intellect projects its false imagination in the states of waking and dreaming and merges in the nescience in the state of deep sleep. 'Just as the water of the mirage does not make the desert wet this unreal thing (world) will not do any harm to me who is its basis.' Such a conviction is real knowledge. This is the means of liberation. I have already said this. Darkness will not disappear through anything except light; it will not disappear through ritualistic acts, meditation (*upāsana*)[1] etc. The darkness of nescience departs along with its effects, from him in whose heart the light of knowledge arises. He remains always as the unattached and homogeneous Self of the form of *Brahman*. Nothing came into existence in the past. Nor is there anything existing now. Nor will there be anything in the future. Since the objects that are known do not (really) exist, the terms 'witness' and 'seer' are not applicable. Since there is no bondage there is no liberation. Since there is no nescience there is no knowledge. He who has known this and cast away the sense of duty is a sage (*jnāni*). Whether his senses come into contact with their objects or not he is unattached and free from desires. Therefore, even though he may appear to act, he does nothing.

Disciple: How can the individual who is of the form of 'I-I' and is numerous and finite and subject to attachment and other forms of misery, be identical with *Brahman* which is one and all-pervasive and free from attachment and other forms of misery? If individual and *Brahman* are the same, who is it that acts? And who bestows the fruits of action?

Guru: Although *Brahman* cannot be identical with the individuality (*jīva*) which is limited to the inner organ (*antahkarana*) and which is the apparent meaning of 'I', it can be with the witness (*sākshi*), which is the implied meaning of the word 'I'. It is the reflected part (*ābhāsa bhāga*) of the *jīva* which performs action. The reflected part in *Isvara* (God), which is the apparent meaning of the word *tat* (*Brahman*), bestows the fruits of action. There is no difference in the consciousness which is the implied meaning of these words (I and *tat*). Nor do these two aspects (*jīva* and *Isvara*) really exist.

Disciple: Who is the *jīva*? Who is the *sākshi* (witness)? Is not a witness other than the *jīva* a sheer impossibility like the son of a barren women?

Guru: Just as the reflection of the sky in a pot becomes the sky in the water, consciousness established in the intellect (*buddhi*) along with the reflected consciousness (*ābhāsa*) in the intellect, accompanied by desires and action, becomes the *jīva* who is the doer, enjoyer and *samsārin*. The consciousness which is the basis of the intellect and which is the attribute of the *jīva* or the finite (*vyasti*) nescience, is the immutable witness (*kutastha*). He has no beginning and is unchanging. Features (*dharmas*) like good and evil, joy and sorrow, going to another world and coming back to this, belong to the reflected consciousness alone. Even in the reflected consciousness they exist only in the inner organ which is its attribute. They do not exist in the consciousness which is the substance part (of the *jīva*). The substance part of the *jīva* is the witness. In one and the same consciousness the inner organ is the adjunct (*upādhi*) for the ideas of witness and attribute for the idea of *jīva*. That is to say, the single consciousness becomes the *jīva* along with the inner organ and the witness when bereft of it. That is, one and the same inner organ is the adjunct of consciousness in the eyes of one who lacks discrimination. Therefore the single consciousness is the witness for a man of discrimination and *jīva* for one who lacks discrimination.

Disciple: How is it possible for even the witness, who is manifold and limited on account of the multiplicity of *jīva*s, to be identical with *Brahman* who is one?

Guru: Just as the space in a pot which is manifold and limited is not different from, and in fact is, the same as total space (*mahākāsa*), the witness who is manifold and limited is not different from *Brahman* but is *Brahman*. It is therefore possible for it to be identical with *Brahman*. Therefore know 'I am *Brahman*'.

Disciple: For whom is this knowledge? For the *jīva* or for the witness?

Guru: Knowledge and ignorance are for the *jīva* alone and not for the witness.

Disciple: Will not the knowledge 'I am *Brahman*' which arises in the *jīva*, which is different from *Brahman*, be false?

Guru: As the immutable Self (*kutastha*) implied in the term 'I' is always one with *Brahman*, like the pot-space and infinite space, it is completely identical with it. As for the *jīva* implied in the term 'I', it can have identity with *Brahman* 'by removal of obstruction' (*bādha samānādhikaranyam*) through negating the idea of *jīva*, just as the man one imagines one sees in a post (in a dim light) becomes one with the post of the negation of the idea of its being a man.

Disciple: Do the reflected consciousness (*ābhāsa*) and the immutable (*kutastha*) which are implied in the term 'I' exist at the same time? Or do they appear at different times?

Guru: They appear at the same time. The reflected consciousness is the object of the witness, but the witness is self-cognized. When there is actual knowledge of pots and other external objects what happens is this: The concept part in the concept of the inner organ accompanied by the reflected consciousness goes out as far as the pots and other objects and assumes their forms and removes the obstruction (*āvaranam*) which naturally covers them, on account of ignorance. Just as a non-luminous object covered by a pot will not be seen (in the dark) even if the pot is broken by a stick, but can be seen with the help of a lamp, even so the reflected part illumines the objects.

When there is direct realization of *Brahman*, which is the Self, what happens is this: The inner organ, with the help of the sound produced by the important scriptural saying (*mahāvākya*)[2] 'That thou art' (*tat tvam asi*) when connected with the ear, takes the form of *Brahman* (*Brahmākāra*) and loses contact with the senses. This is like the knowledge of the tenth man (*dasama*) which arises through the sound produced by the sentence 'you are the tenth man', or like the ideas of joy and sorrow which arise without any (corresponding) external objects. This concept of the form of *Brahman* removes the obstruction hiding the Self and then the slight ignorance which still persists in the inner organ disappears like the dirt (in a cloth) which is removed by soap. Thereafter *Brahman* becomes manifest by his own effulgence like the light of the glorious sun which shines when slight obstructions like one's fingers held over one's eyes are removed. Just as a lamp kept in a pot shines without the aid of another light when the pot is broken, *Brahman* too does not require the help of the reflected consciousness.

Disciple: What are the chief (*antaranga*) and secondary (*bahiranga*) means of attaining this knowledge?

Guru: Ritualistic sacrifices and similar acts and meditation (*upāsana*) performed without motive are the secondary means. The four (qualifications)[3] like discrimination, the three (steps)[4] and (the one) enquiry into the meaning of 'That' and 'Thou'; these eight make up the chief means.

Disciple: If knowledge arises through the 'saying' alone, where is the need for 'hearing' etc?

Guru: Knowledge is of two kinds, namely steady (free from defects) and unsteady (defective). Although an inferior aspirant (*mandādhikāri*) who has doubts and false notions may have direct knowledge through the teaching of the 'saying' it will not produce the proper effect, it is defective. By constant practice of 'hearing' etc, the defect will be removed. This is the aim of 'hearing' etc. In the case of a superior aspirant (*uttama adhikāri*) whose inner organ is extremely pure and free from the doubts and false notions, so that steady direct knowledge will arise by merely hearing the saying. It is not necessary to have hearing, etc, (again) for removing the defects. He alone is 'liberated while alive' (*jīvan mukta*), whose wisdom is firm (*sthita prajna*).

Disciple: What are the distinguishing marks of the sage and the ignorant person?

Guru: The ignorant person is distinguished by his attachment (*rāga*), the sage by dispassion. Even if the ignorant person occasionally develops dispassion, it is likely to change since he has not got rid of the sense of reality in the objects of the senses. His dispassion is superficial. On the other hand, the dispassion of the sage, which has developed out of his sense of the unreality of objects of the senses, does not change at any time and is therefore intense.

Disciple: Why do some persons say that ritualistic acts (*karma*) accompanied by meditation (*upāsana*) and knowledge (*jnāna*) are the cause of steadiness?

Guru: The idea that the Self, which is separate from the body, is the doer and enjoyer and the idea that the doer, the act and its result are different from one another, are the cause of ritualistic acts; the result is impermanent *samsāra*. The Self is of the nature of the unattached *Brahman*; the doer, the act and the result are not distinct from the Self; this is knowledge, and its fruit is eternal liberation. So how can these two co-exist?

Disciple: So long as the inner organ exists its natural quality of unsteadiness will not leave even the sage. Therefore if it is not an obstacle to liberation after death (*videha mukti*) how can there be the experience of bliss of liberation while alive? Is it not necessary for even the sage to meditate (do *upāsana*) in order to remove the unsteadiness of the mind?

Guru: Since *samādhi* and distraction are the same to a sage of steadfast wisdom, he does not enter into any action for the sake of steadiness of mind. For him there is no nescience as a cause of his activity, nor any delusion of difference as a result of nescience, nor attachment and hatred resulting from the delusion of difference. Only *prārabdha* (that part of one's *karma* which has to be worked out in this life) remains: this is the cause of his activity. And that being different from person to person, there is no fixity (*lit.* order) in regard to the activity arising out of *prārabdha*. Hence the sage's activity and inactivity are governed by *prārabdha*. Therefore there can be desire for sense-enjoyment and efforts to attain it, as in the case of Janaka and others, on account of the *prārabdha* responsible for enjoyment. Similarly, there can be the desire for liberation while alive, and disgust with sense-enjoyment as in the case of Suka, Vāmadeva and others, on account of the *prārabdha* responsible for inactivity. The bliss of *Brahman* will not become manifest owing to the mere immobility of the inner organ. It will become manifest only through the concept of the form of *Brahman* (*Brahmākāra vritti*). Since this will arise only through reflection (*chintana*) on the meaning of the *Vēdānta* (texts), and since unsteadiness will disappear even through this, one who desires to have the bliss of liberation while alive has to reflect on the meaning of *Vēdānta* texts only and need not meditate (do *upāsana*).

Disciple: Can the sage have too much activity?

Guru: When activity is excessive, happiness will decrease; when activity is less, the happiness will be more. But knowledge remains the same. Although activity is inimical to that (kind of) happiness which is distinct from liberation while alive, it is not inimical to liberation while alive, since there is not delusion of bondage by activity and inactivity so far as the Self is concerned.

Disciple: Since the sage cannot have attachment on account of his seeing all objects as non-Self, unreal and evil, what can motivate his activity?

Guru: Although he knows the body to be unreal, the sage may be active on account of his *prārabdha*; for instance, he may go begging, etc, to maintain the body on account of his *prārabdha*. It is like people watching a conjuring act even when they know how it is done, or like an invalid doing things that are bad for him even though he knows that they are.

Disciple: What is the meaning of saying that the sage has no desires?

Guru: It is not that his inner organ will not take the form of desires. As the inner organ is not the product of pure *sattva* alone, but of the less prominent *rajas* and *tamas*, in combination with the prominent *sattva*, all the qualities will more or less exist in it. Therefore, so long as the inner organ remains there will not be entire absence of desires which are modifications of *rajas*. But the sage does not mistake the desires for characteristics of the Self. That is the difference. He is unattached. Though he acts he is a non-doer. That is why the scripture (*sruti*) says that the good and bad acts done by the body and the merit and demerit (acquired thereby) after attaining knowledge do not affect him.

Disciple: Is it not necessary for the sage to enter into blissful and non-dual *nirvikalpa samādhi* in which concepts are all absorbed in nescience, as in deep sleep, and there is no experience of nescience-covered bliss and the concept of the inner organs in the form of *Brahman* (*Brahmākāra vritti*) is absorbed in the effulgence of *Brahman*?

On hearing this the Guru laughed thinking, 'Why does he talk like a fool?'

Disciple: Won't one who, while alive, gives up the bliss of liberation to enjoy sense pleasures, give up liberation after death for the desire to attain heavenly worlds?

Guru: The rejection of the bliss of liberation while alive and the desire for worldly enjoyments may happen in the case of a sage on account of his *prārabdha*, but they will not happen after his nescience is burnt up by his knowledge. Therefore his life force (*prāna*) will not go out and he cannot become embodied again either in this world or any other on account of *prārabdha*. Hence the rejection of liberation after death and desire for, or attainment of, other worlds is not possible for the sage.

Disciple: What is liberation while alive? And what is liberation after death?

Guru: The absence of the delusion of bondage even while one is embodied, is liberation while alive. The absorption of the gross and subtle nescience in consciousness after the experience of *prārabdha* is liberation after death.

This is the gist of the important scriptural texts.

On hearing this the disciple experienced the direct knowledge of his Self and, after first experiencing liberation while alive, attained liberation after death.

OM TAT SAT

Sri Ramanārpanamasthu

II

RAMANA MAHARSHI'S
FORTY VERSES
ON
REALITY

PREFACE

It was not without much hesitation that I acceded to the suggestion of one or two of my friends to prepare a simplified translation of Sri Bhagavan's ULLADU NARPADU, or *Forty Verses on Reality*, which newcomers to Sri Ramanasram, especially the English-speaking foreigners who come in increasing numbers, might more easily understand.

It is generally admitted that Sri Bhagavan's ideas are often beyond the reach of the common reader and the beginner. They are made more difficult by his Tamil mode of expression and by the spontaneity with which he wrote the individual verses, for it was not his intention to produce a compact philosophical system or thesis. He wrote the verses as they occurred to him, and they were later arranged by a disciple in the order in which we see them in print.

When undertaking this venture I placed before me six different English translations, chose the versions common to the majority of them, and wrote these down in an almost conversational English. I avoided technical terms and difficult words so far as this could be done while remaining faithful to the original. When I had a doubt due to lack of agreement between the different translators, I sought the help of Tamil scholars in Vellore.

I also wrote brief notes on each verse, developing the verse's main points so that in some places the notes read like a paraphrase, but without learned quotations or long dissertations. For all that the seekers (*sadhakas*) need and want is to understand the spirit of Bhagavan's utterances and apply it in their spiritual practice (*sadhana*).

In these forty verses, as the reader will observe, Bhagavan has touched on all the salient points of his teaching, constantly stressing the great value and efficacy of the *vichāra*, or investigation into the nature of the investigator himself. All the Masters of the Upanishads maintain that man is not the elements out of which his body is made, but the mind, or intelligent principle, or being, which uses the body. *That* is the serene, blissful Self, the absolute, secondless Reality, which all are seeking consciously and unconsciously in different ways — devious or straight, wrong or right — and of which the *sadhaka* endeavours to have a direct and full Knowledge.

The synopsis which follows not only gives the gist of every verse, but is also intended to help the reader to locate a specific subject. It takes the place of an index, which seems out of place in a small work like this.

S. S. Cohen

SYNOPSIS

Invocation

**i. Without awareness of Reality, can Reality exist?
Because this awareness-reality, itself free from thought,
exists as the source of all thoughts, it is called Heart.
How to know it? To be as it is (thought-free) in the Heart,
is to know it.**

This verse and the next form the Invocation, which customarily
precedes spiritual and poetic works in Indian literature. It may be
addressed to a particular deity such as Ganapati, the *deva* in
charge of poetic effusions, or to the *devas* in general, to a
favourite *devi*, or to the guru or to one or other of the three major
divinities. But Bhagavan, recognising a single Reality from which
all things proceed, makes his dedication to that, as the pure
Awareness (*chit*) abiding in the Heart as eternal existence (*sat*), or
the absolute Brahman.

The literal translation of the first sentence of this verse reads:
'Can there be awareness of that which is other than existence?' This
makes knowledge or awareness the criterion of existence, because
the non-existent cannot make itself known. The colour, for
example, that is not visible, or the sound that is not audible,
amounts to nothing. Should however something non-existent be
perceived, like the water in a mirage, or the figure of a man in a
wooden post, it cannot but be an appearance, a misleading thought
in the perceiving consciousness. For the absolutely real alone exists
absolutely, and the apparent has no existence whatever.

But here is may be asked that since both the Real and the
apparently real are cognisable, how is one to distinguish between
them? The former is changeless and exists (eternally) as the

knower, which is always a subject and never an object; whereas the latter, being a mere thought, ceaselessly changes and is insentient, always an object and never a subject. Close study will reveal that the external world — that is every perceived object and every thought and sensation — is an unreal, dream-like appearance.

As for the Real, although it is not so easily recognisable, yet, according to this verse it is certainly knowable. If so, 'how to know it?' Bhagavan asks and gives some clues regarding its nature in order to lead the seekers to it: it is pure awareness, it dwells in the Heart, nay, it is the Heart itself; it is the source of all thoughts, itself being free from thoughts, and so forth. From this we must infer that Reality is not only consciousness, but also changeless. It is itself free from changing thoughts. Thoughts emanate from it, and, like shadows cast on it, obstruct our view of it, so that to have an immediate apprehension of it we have to part from all thoughts and remain, like it, in our native purity in the heart — 'thought-free'.

As we proceed we shall see Bhagavan developing his theme that the *vichāra*, or enquiry, is the easiest method by which one can attain this objective of *jnāna*, or knowledge of the absolute reality which is one's own Self.

This one verse sets the keynote for the whole work, like the *sruti* or the continuous base note in music. Readers will do well to keep it always in mind in their study of the other verses.

ii. Those who have an infinite fear of death take refuge in the Feet of the supreme Lord Who is without birth and death. Can the thought of death occur to those who have destroyed their 'I' and 'mine' and have become immortal?

Those who most identify themselves with the body are the people who fear death most. Seeing the dissolution of the body they deduce their own dissolution to be simultaneous with it, and dread the terrible Unknown that lurks behind it. Their only hope of safety lies, therefore, in the worship of the Almighty Lord, who alone is deathless.

But those who through the practice of *sadhana* or spiritual discipline have transcended this false identification no longer have bodies to be the victims of death. Even the thought of death does not occur to them. They are *videhas*, bodiless, although they continue to occupy a body.

This verse also implies that by taking refuge in the Lord, these fear-torn people will, in course of time, so progress spiritually that they will be able to destroy their sense of 'I' and 'mine' and attain immortality, since the death of the ego will evidently destroy death and the thought of death.

Text

1. Because the world is seen, we have to infer a common cause (a Lord) possessing unlimited powers to appear as the diversity. The pictures consisting of names and forms, the seer, the canvas, the light – all these are He Himself.

The 'Forty' begins here. To understand Bhagavan's meaning we have to use the key with which he supplies us in the Invocation. There he declares Reality to be the thought-free Awareness which dwells in the heart. Here he brings in the world in order to meet on their own ground those disciples who do perceive a 'real', external world. He is saying something like this: 'You see a world and ascribe an omnipotent creator to it. But as we have already seen, this creation is only an appearance, a manifestation of that Awareness of which we were speaking. It has no more reality in itself than have the pictures projected on a screen.' From the heart thoughts spontaneously rise, like vapour from the ocean, and turn into a kaleidosopic world of names, forms, colours, sounds, smells and other impressions. These are in it, or on it as on a canvas of which the heart is itself the seer and the sight.

Pure Consciousness or Pure Mind is thus the pictures, the screen, the seer, and the light or sight.

2. All schools of thought postulate the fundamental triad — God, soul and world — although all three are manifestations of the One. The belief that the three remain eternally three lasts only as long as the 'I' or ego lasts. To destroy the ego and remain in one's own state is best.

Most religions are based on the assumption that the triad mentioned in the text is eternal. Bhagavan rejects this assumption as being the child of the ignorant ego which mistakes itself for the body. The 'I-am-the-body' notion compels the admission of an individuality (*jīva*), a world, and its creator, as three distinct, perennial, co-existing entities. Bhagavan, as we have seen, perceives a single existence of which these three are an illusory manifestation which, however, vanishes the moment the eternal 'I' is apprehended and the ego perishes.

3. Of what avail to debate whether the world is real and unreal, sentient or insentient, pleasant or unpleasant? Extinguishing the ego, transcending the world, realising the Self — that is the state which is dear to all, and free from the sense of unity and duality.

The same line of thought continues. Destruction of the ego is a *sine qua non* for the realisation of the Self within the heart. It brings to an end all speculation about reality and unreality, God and world, whose true nature will be revealed in actual experience. This is the most blissful attainable state and beyond the plurality of the illusory world.

4. If the Self be with form, God and the world will be also. If one be formless oneself, how and by whom can their forms be seen? Can there be sight without eyes? The Self is the eye, the limitless Eye.

This refers to the *jnāni*, who although having a body sees himself as bodiless and formless, and so cannot see God, or in fact see anything with form. The *ajnani* (the non-realised), perceiving himself as a body, takes God also to be a body and worships him in all sorts of material, formal representations. Yet the fact remains that even he perceives everything through his own formless Self, which we have granted to be the only seer, the only knowledge there is – the 'limitless Eye'. Those who condemn idol-worship forget that they themselves worship material symbols and icons, and attribute to God forms, dimensions, positions, even sentiments and sense-perceptions exactly as they do to themselves. Having no experience or conception of a formless omniscient spirit, they feel literally lost at the idea of worshipping something not represented in a form. God, thus, appears according to the degree of the realisation of one's Self.

'Can there be sight without eyes?' means that without consciousness there can be no knowledge of anything, just as without a lamp none of the objects present in a dark room can be seen. Can there be a world to an unconscious man?

5. The body is in the form of, and includes, the five sheaths. Is there a world apart from the body? Has anyone without a body seen the world?

The body is a complex structure containing a large number of instruments or organs which the Self, as ego, uses for a large number of purposes, including among others those of hearing, smelling, seeing, thinking, feeling, memorising and reasoning. The materials out of which these instruments or parts are made vary from the grossest to the finest. The *Shastras* (the Scriptures) have arranged them in five groups. To each group one sheath or *kosha* is assigned. The *kosha* dealing with purely physical matter is called *annamayakosha* (the sheath of food). The *pranamayakosha* (the vital sheath) looks after the fivefold functions of the vital energies — breathing, assimilation, generation, excretion and locomotion. The *manomayakosha* (mental sheath) contains the faculties of mentation. The *vijñānamayakosha* is the sheath of the intellectual and reasoning faculties, of scientific and philo-sophical thinking, and last is the *anandamayakosha*, the sheath of bliss, or causal sheath, which stores up within itself the karmic seeds of every birth and is concerned with that state in which profound peace is enjoyed by the dreamless sleeper. This *kosha* is made of the finest substance, *sattva*, which in itself is happy, due to its freedom from grossness and to its close proximity to the blissful Self.

Thus the term body includes all these *koshas*, whose appearance and disappearance cause the appearance and disappearance of all objective and subjective perceptions. Assumption of a body is therefore necessary for the world's enjoyment and the body owes its existence, as we shall see in the next verse, to the five senses, which are the properties of the mind.

6. The world is but the fivefold sense-objects, which are the results of the five senses. Since the mind perceives the world through the senses, is there a world without the mind?

Through the sensory organs lodged in the five *koshas*, the senses display before the mind a variety of objects — physical, vital, emotional, mental and intellectual. Apart from the five sense-perceptions, there are all sorts of other internal senses which also arise from the mind, work through the mind, and are understood by the mind — such as the senses of time, of space, of 'I' and 'mine', and the artistic, ethical, religious and spiritual senses for instance. Since all these senses form the world we know and have one common origin, which is the mind, the world cannot therefore be other than that mind.

7. Although the world and the awareness of it rise and set together, it is by awareness that the world is known. The source from which they both rise, and into which they set, always shines without itself rising or setting. That alone is real.

This verse is reminiscent of the Invocation and confirms the previous verse, which make awareness the criterion of existence as well as the source of the world. Awareness 'always shines' as the 'limitless Eye' mentioned in verse four, the external Knower. It goes without saying that the appearance of the world is simultaneous with the awareness of it, and disappearance of the world simultaneous with the withdrawal of that awareness. For the fact of the awareness of the world is the fact of its existence. We cannot affirm the existence of an object without first affirming awareness of it. Therefore awareness is the only Reality there is.

8. In whatever name and form the nameless and formless is worshipped, therein lies the path of its realisation. Realising one's truth as the truth of that reality, and merging into it, is true realisation.

All roads lead to Rome – all sincere worship comes from the heart, and leads to the formless God in the heart. To believe that one's reality is the same as God's is an important step towards the realisation of Him as Pure Consciousness and the process of merging into Him. How many millions of innocent human beings would have been spared the horror of religious persecutions throughout the centuries in the name of God, and how many wars would have been prevented, had this truth been accepted as the one truth underlying all religions, the basic world faith!

9. The dyads and triads rest on the basic One. Enquiring about that One in the mind, they will disappear. Those who see thus are the seers of truth: they remain unruffled.

The dyads are the pairs of opposites – knowledge and ignorance, light and darkness, happiness and misery, birth and death, etc. The triad is the triple principle of seen, seer and sight; object, subject and the perception of the former by the latter. As all the numbers stand on, and originate from, the first number, so are the dyads and triads based on, arising from, and of the same nature as the one seer, the perceiving mind. He who realises the world as such retains a uniform serenity in all conditions of life.

10. Knowledge and ignorance are inter-related: the one does not exist without the other. Enquiring to whom is that knowledge and that ignorance, and arriving at their root cause, the Self, this is true knowledge.

To speak of ignorance is to admit its opposite – knowledge – and *vice versa*. Until we become aware of an object we remain ignorant of its existence. To learn a lesson is to admit our previous ignorance of its content. Knowledge is thus the light which clears away the darkness of ignorance. But knowledge and ignorance which pertain to external objects are mere modes of thought. They come and go, and are therefore of no consequence in the search for Truth. What is of consequence is their knower, who is fixed, changeless, also called first principle because he is efficient, causeless, the eternal thinker, who precedes and survives all his thoughts — 'the basic One' (verse nine).

11. Is it not ignorance to know all but the all-knowing Self? When the latter, the substratum of both knowledge and ignorance, is known, knowledge and ignorance themselves both disappear.

It is of course foolish to know about everything in the world, and remain ignorant of one's own Self. Knowledge of the perishable — the universe and all its contents — perishes with the body, and cannot be transferred to another body, except perhaps as tendencies or abilities in the perishable too, which may not have any spiritual value in a future life. The imperishable alone endures and gives imperishable satisfaction, and this lies wholly within ourselves, who are the source and ground of both knowledge and ignorance — that is, of all experiences whatever.

12. True knowledge is neither knowledge nor ignorance. Objective knowledge is not true knowledge. Because the Self is self-effulgent, having no second to know or be known, it is Supreme Knowledge — not empty nothingness.

This continues the theme of verses ten and eleven. We have seen that objective knowledge is knowledge of the perishable, the apparent, the non-existent, the unreal (see Invocation). Self-awareness is true knowledge, because it is absolute, i.e. changeless, non-dual, ever-pure (thought-free). This purity is not emptiness (because of the lack of perceivable objects in it), but the ever-shining plenum of Awareness-Being (*chit-Sat*).

13. The Self alone is knowledge, is truth. Knowledge of the diversity is ignorance, is false knowledge. Yet ignorance is not apart from the Self, which is knowledge. Are the ornaments different from the gold which is real?

So the world with all its multiplicity of shapes, colours, smells, tastes and so forth is nothing but pure consciousness in substance, like variously-shaped jewellery which is nothing but gold. To perceive shapes, colours, smells and the like as different from one another is ignorance, is illusion, but to see them as the single substance out of which they are made — the pure mind — is true knowledge.

   'Yet ignorance is not apart from the Self' because all experiences as thoughts come from the Self and are witnessed by it (verses six and seven).

14. The 'I' existing, 'you' and 'he' also exist. If by investigating the truth of the 'I' the 'I' ceases, 'you' and 'he' will also cease and will shine as the One. This is the natural state of one's being.

'You' and 'he' are the world; it stands and falls with the 'I' or ego, which constructs it. Realising one's being is realising the whole world to be the same effulgent being — 'the One'. This state of being is experienced by the Self-realised man in the waking state consciously, and by all men in dreamless sleep. In dreamless sleep (*sushupti*) the 'I', like everything else, disappears, and one remains in one's native state - in the true 'I' – but generally without retaining memory of this condition on awakening.

15. On the present the past and the future stand. They too are the present in their times. Thus the present alone exists. Ignoring the present, and seeking to know the past and the future, is like trying to count without the initial unit.

The present *is* always, for even the past was the present in its time, and so also will the future be the present in *its* time. Whatever happens therefore happens only in the present. When Methuselah was born, he was born in the present, and when he died after nine or ten centuries he died also in the present, despite the later date. Similarly all that happened to him between those two events happened also in the present. Thus the present is the only significant tense in actuality. Moreover, let us not forget the fact that time is made of instants which are so minute as to have no room either for a past or for a future, but for the present alone. The next verse will tell us that even the present is unreal, being one of the notions of our mind, as past and future are – acts of our memory.

16. Do time and space exist apart from us? If we are the body we are affected by time and space. But are we the body? We are the same now, then, and for ever.

Of course time and space are mere concepts in us. Because in our long journey in life we pass through multitudes of experiences, we have to conceive past, present and future in order to arrange them conveniently in their sequence of occurrence in our memory. Because we perceive multiplicity, we have to conceive a space in which to accommodate them, like the screen on which cinematograph pictures are spread. Without a screen there can be no pictures. The screen on which the universe actually appears and moves is thus our own mind, from which it emanates as thoughts, either of external physical objects, or of internal concepts, sensations, emotions, including the senses of time and space.

Those who take themselves for the body take *time* to be the creator and destroyer of all things, and thus it inspires them with great fear — fear of future calamities, of death, of loss of fortune and position, or whatever it may be. Many of them consult astrologers to read the decrees of time and foretell events long in advance of their occurrence. To them birth, youth, old age and death; creation, preservation and dissolution; past, present and future; health and disease, prosperity and adversity all exist without the shadow of a doubt: they fall prey to time and its vagaries. The others who know themselves to be pure spirit are bodiless, timeless and spaceless; and, Bhagavan affirms, they are thus free from the hallucination of: 'We alone are.' Time and space are not.

17. To those who have not realised the Self, as well as to those who have, the body is 'I'. To the former the 'I' is only of the size of the body; whereas to those who have realised the Self within the body, the 'I' shines without limits. This is the difference between the two.

The *jnāni* (the Self-realised) like everybody else, refers to the body as 'I'. Whereas the others confine their 'I' to the flesh-and-body and to its height and breath, the *jnāni* takes his 'I' to be the life which pervades the body as well as the limitless space outside it. Realisation is the direct and undubitable proof of this truth.

18. To those who have realised the Self and to those who have not, the world is real. To the latter its reality is confined to the spatial measurements of the world, whereas to the former it is formless, and shines as the substratum of the world. This is the difference between the two.

The space which the world occupies is the limit of its reality to the ignorant (*ajnani*), but to the *jnāni* it is the limitless substratum of the world. Science tells us that space is not material, that is, it is not made of atoms and molecules, like the objects which occupy it, to be visible to the eye. The perception of space by the eye is the worst illusion men suffer. Space is a mental concept, i.e. it is a projection *by the mind to make the reality of the world plausible*. If space is a concept, so should be the objects that occupy it, notwithstanding their atoms and molecules. All the universes and galaxies in the Cosmos are made of atoms and nothing else. But what are the atoms after all but the indestructible absolute energy? The *jnani* experiences this energy as the pure intelligence that is himself. The absolute Reality is thus absolute energy as well as absolute consciousness – *Sat* as well as *Chit* – omnipotent, omnipresent as well as omniscient, the world as well as the creator and seer of the world.

19. Disputations as to which prevails over the other, fate or free will, are for those who have no knowledge of the Self, which is the ground of both fate and free will. Those who have realised this ground are free from both. Will they be caught by them again?

Fate or destiny is *karma*. *Karma*, like free will, is unintelligent, and can thus affect only the unintelligent in man, namely, the body, and not the intelligent being, who is the lord of the body. When realisation of this being is achieved, *karma* and free will will have no feet to stand on and will crumble to dust of their own accord.

The scholars do not worry over whether destiny and free will affect the individual or his body, but argue about which of them dominates the other in its operation. Our own approach to this question is simple. We exercise our will freely and let *karma* take care of itself. Vasishta Muni exhorts Rama to make constant efforts in his *sadhana* and forget all about the complexities of destiny. He compares *karma* and free will to two battling rams, of which the stronger will always win in the end. Thus strong efforts will overcome destiny.

Some theorists stretch themselves so far as to believe that even the exercise of the will is predestined, that is, destiny is always dominant, leaving no room for freedom of the will. If they are right then religion, ethical conduct, obedience to moral laws, service of man and humane actions are wasted effort, and evil-doing will be on a par with virtuous deeds. Moreover, men would be no better than machines which produce what is put into them, or than animals which are not responsible for their actions and thus, not liable to punishment or reward. Fortunately it is not so: the admission of punishment and reward, which is the funda-mental condition in the operation of *karma*, inevitably leads to the admission of free will. Karma begins to operate only after the will has been exercised *ad libitum*. The genesis is free will not *karma*, which follows it like its shadow.

20. Without seeing the Self, the seeing of God is a mental image. Seeing the Self is seeing God, they say. Completely losing the ego and seeing the Self is finding God; for the Self is not other than God.

The great Western religions hold that the question whether there is a God other than man is sacrilegious. The supremacy of God over man, they argue, is so self-evident that the very question is derogatory to God Almighty. Bhagavan answers the question in the negative because, whereas the Western theologians take man to be the merest dust, the corruptible body, Bhagavan takes him to be the spirit or life within the body, which is infinite and eternal.

These who have no experience of the Self but claim to have seen God, Bhagavan asserts, have seen only their own mental picture of God resembling their own physical picture more or less, having a shape, colour, size, etc. which God the pure Spirit simply does not have.

21. The Scriptures declare that seeing the Self is seeing God. Being single, how can one see one's own Self? If Oneself cannot be seen, how can God be? To be absorbed by God is to see Him.

God is the Self, we said, but 'how to see one's own Self', which has no second to perceive or reflect it? Here seeing the Self is knowing the Self, the Self being pure knowledge, itself the seer and itself the seen. Knower and known are thus one and the same being. Therefore seeing God is being dissolved in God or Self.

'Being single' draws attention to the freedom of man from his *upādhis* (adjuncts), which are anything but 'single' with their *koshas*, organs, faculties, and their manifold qualities such as shape, size, colour, smell and taste. Therefore, to be himself, that is to be 'single', man the ego has to shed all these superfluities which he has been mistaking for himself, and remain as consciousness in the heart. *That* is the true vision or true being of God.

22. The Lord shines within the mind, illuminating it. Unless it turn inward and be fixed in the Lord, it is not possible for the mind to know Him.

Mind here is *jīva* which, working through its *manas* (the faculty of the lower intellect), perceives the world and remains always preoccupied with it. Being an intelligent knower, the *jīva* is not other than the Lord Himself, but because it is in constant contact with the world, it can have no knowledge of Him, or, what is the same, of itself. To have this knowledge, all it has to do is to turn its attention inwards to the Heart, where the Lord is seated. This is the same as renouncing the adjuncts mentioned in the last note.

23. The body does not say 'I'. In sleep no one admits he is not. The 'I' emerging, all else emerges. Enquire with a keen mind whence this 'I' rises.

The body, being insentient, knows nothing about 'I' and 'not-I', yet the 'I' persists with or without a body – in the waking state or in sleep or swoon – as the man who himself wakes, swoons, and sleeps. When he wakes up the whole world wakes up, and when he sleeps the whole world sleeps. To know the true nature of this perennial 'I', we have to conduct an enquiry into its source.

24. The insentient body does not say 'I'. The ever-existent consciousness is not born (thus cannot say 'I'). The 'I' of the size of the body springs up between the two: it is known as *chit-jada-granthi* (the knot which ties together the sentient and insentient), bondage, individuality, ego, subtle body, *samsāra*, mind, etc.

The body, unaware of its own existence, does not say 'I'; and the Self which is pure spirit, pure intelligence, has never come to birth and so, also, does not say 'I'. But somehow the intelligence, under the compelling power of *avidya* (ignorance) assumes a body, comes to identify itself with this body and to call itself 'I', thus tying together body and soul in a knot, which is known as the knot of ignorance in the heart – literally the sentience-insentience knot. It is an extremely hard knot which defies centuries of births, but breaks of its own accord when Self-realisation is achieved, and bondage and ignorance are destroyed for ever.

'*Samsāra*' means going round on the wheel of birth and death. In India the wife is significantly also called *samsāra*.

25. Know that this formless ghost (the ego of 'I') springs up in a form (body). Taking a form it lives, feeds and grows. Leaving a form it picks up another, but when it is enquired into, it drops the form and takes to flight.

The ego is a veritable ghost. A ghost is a disembodied spirit that takes on a shadowy appearance to play the living being and hoax people. The ego also is formless spirit – the *Atman* itself – but it picks up a body and, without knowing it, hoaxes others as well as itself. It begins its *samsaric* career by identifying itself with the body to enjoy the good things of the world. It reaps the retribution of falling into abysmal *avidya* (ignorance), losing memory of its true nature, and acquiring the false notions of having a birth, of acting, eating and growing, of accumulating wealth, marrying and begetting children, of being diseased, hungry and miserable and finally, of dying. But when the time of its redemption draws near, it undertakes an investigation into its real nature, sheds its identification with the body, transcends its previous illusions and becomes free once again, full of the bliss of self-discovery and self-knowledge (*jnāna*).

26. The ego existing, all else exists. The ego not existing nothing else exists. The ego is thus all. Enquiring as to what the ego is, is therefore surrendering all.

Verse fourteen also makes the ego, or 'I' the all. But here, we are led to draw the conclusion that true surrender is the surrender of the ego (which is the totality of the not-Self, of 'everything') and that the same surrender can be achieved by the method of *vichāra* spoken of before.

27. The non-emergence of the 'I' is the state of being THAT. Without seeking and attaining the place whence the 'I' emerges, how is one to achieve self-extinction — the non-emergence of the 'I'? Without that achievement, how is one to abide as THAT — one's true state?

The non-emergence of the 'I' means ego-lessness, the natural state of being or THAT. To stop the ego from rising we have to find the place of its emergence and annihilate it there, before it emerges, so that we may consciously ever abide as THAT, egoless, in the heart, as we unconsciously do in deep sleep. The word 'place' stands here for Heart.

28. Like the diver who dives to recover what has fallen into deep water, controlling speech and breath and with a keen mind, one must dive into himself and find whence the 'I' emerges.

The basic theme of many of the previous verses, it must have been observed, is the *vichāra*, through which the search for the ego's source has to be made. Deep diving is a metaphor that implies salvaging the ego from the depths of ignorance into which it has fallen, not amateurishly but very expertly and unremittingly, or else success will be sporadic and even doubtful. Bhagavan means that this *sadhak's* life should be dedicated to Realisation and to nothing else, for who knows what obstacles destiny will raise against him to bar his march to the highest in future lives? So he asks us to turn into divers right now, controlling speech and breath. Breath-control is equivalent to mental silence (suspension of thoughts), which has to be practised alongside the enquiry in order to train the mind to be alone, *kaivalya* ('thought-free'), when it will perceive itself in its natural purity, the most precious Self, 'whence the 'I' emerges.'

29. Seeking the source of the 'I' with a mind turned inwards and no uttering of the word 'I' is indeed the path of knowledge. Meditation on 'I am not this, I am that' is an aid to the enquiry, but not the enquiry itself.

Bhagavan misses no opportunity of reminding us that the quest 'who am I?' is not a formula to be repeated mechanically like an incantation, but an intellectual enquiry into the nature of the 'I' which is carried out until its base is fully grasped and its source is reached. The whole process is dialectical, involving the exercise of the logical faculty, till it ends in the silence of the heart, which transcends all faculties. Some suggestive formula such as 'I am THAT' may be used to begin with, but in course of time it has to turn into an unshakable conviction, side by side with the stilling of the mind as mentioned in the previous commentary, which gradually grows in depth and duration. That is why the path of the *vichāra* is known as the path of knowledge (*jnāna marga*).

30. Enquiring 'Who am I?' within the mind, and reaching the heart, the 'I' collapses. Instantly the real 'I' appears (as 'I' 'I'), which, although it manifests itself as 'I' is not the ego, but the true being.

What happens to the 'I' which has found its own source and collapsed? The meaning is that the 'I' which has not been aware of its own reality has now, through enquiry, come face to face with it, and has turned from the notion of being a mortal body to the realisation of being the shining sea of consciousness. This is the 'collapse' of the false 'I' giving place to the true 'I', which is eternally present as 'I', 'I', 'I' without end or beginning. We must not forget that there is only one, secondless 'I', whether we view it as ego, totally sunk in the pleasures of the world and in ignorance, or as Self, the substratum and source of the world.

'Enquiring within the mind Who am I?' is an affirmation once again, that the quest has to be carried out with the mind.

31. What remains to be done by him, who, having extinguished the ego, remains immersed in the bliss of the Self? He is aware of nothing but the Self. Who can understand his state?

The purpose of all human endeavours, conscious or un-conscious, is the gaining of happiness. The unwise seeks it outside himself in wealth, matrimony, high political and social positions, fame, worldly achievements and pleasure of all sorts. The wise knows that the happiness that comes from an outside cause is illusory due to its precarious nature and its inability even temporarily to confer contentment without trouble, fear, and endless anxiety. Lasting, undiluted happiness is one's very nature, and thus within the grasp of anyone who earnestly seeks it. One who has gained this inner beatitude has no further actions to do, nor purpose to achieve. All his aspirations having been fulfilled, his sole preoccupation remains that ocean of bliss, which passes the understanding of the common man.

32. Despite the Vedas proclaiming 'Thou art THAT', it is sheer weak-mindedness not to investigate into the nature of oneself and abide as the Self, but instead to go on thinking 'THAT I am, not this.'

The main point of this verse is that when the Vedas tell us that we are THAT, we are in duty bound to conduct an enquiry into ourselves in order to experience *the truth of it* and abide as THAT or the Self, rather than just mechanically thinking that we are not the body but THAT. Investigation and meditation will eventually rise above the body-thought, and will reach the *tanumanasi* state (the rarified mind) through which the pure awareness can be directly apprehended. This is the silent heart itself.

33. It is ludicrous to think 'I know myself', or 'I do not know myself', admitting thereby two selves, one the object of the other. That the Self is only one is the experience of all.

To know a thing is to create a duality – the knower and the known. But in self-knowledge there can be no duality, the known being the knower himself, the object and the subject being one and the same identity.

It is common experience that the 'I' is unqualified and single:

it is neither divisible into parts nor tainted by qualities. However fat or lean, old or young, learned or ignorant, rich or poor, whole or dismembered one may be, one is aware of oneself only as 'I' devoid of any attributes. The bare 'I', 'I', 'I' is the primary cognition of everyone, preceding the 'mine' cognition, the body and all its appurtenances, and all its thoughts. This shows that the Self is non-dual, homogeneous and indivisible, and can abide pure by itself with no thoughts to disturb it, being itself not a thought, but the intuitive recognition of oneself as the eternal knower, the pivot — more correctly, the substance — of all one knows. It is evident that the 'I' being pure indivisible consciousness, is experienced by the *jnāni* as the same in all.

34. Without trying to realise in the heart that reality which is the true nature of all, and without trying to abide in it, to engage in disputations as to whether the reality exists or not, or is real or not, denotes delusion born of ignorance.

The theme of the previous verse continues. The realisation of one's Self is the realisation of the true nature of all else, the Self being single and homogeneous. Disputations deepen the ignorance and not infrequently lead to acrimony, anger, hatred, and jealousy among the disputants, not to speak of the vanity and arrogance they create in the hearts of the winners. They should thus be shunned by seekers of Truth and of Peace everlasting.

35. To seek and abide in that which is always attained is true attainment. All other attainments, such as *siddhis* (thaumaturgic powers), are like those acquired in dreams, which prove to be unreal on waking. Can they who are

established in reality and are rid of illusions be ensnared by them?

Sometimes we dream that we are flying in the air, or leaping over precipices hundreds of feet wide, or stopping a running motor car with a light touch of the hand, or doing things which, in the waking state, would appear miraculous, yet prove unreal on waking. The *siddhis* exhibited in the waking state appear to the man who has freed himself from illusion exactly like the dream miracles – utterly false. The greatest of all miracles and all *siddhis* is the discovery of and eternal abidance in, oneself.

In olden days occasionally a *siddhi*-mad youth used to come to Ramanashram with the intention of using Bhagavan's presence to promote the success of his pursuit of *siddhis*. One or two of them were reasonable enough to listen to the advice of the devotees and quit the Ashram betimes. But one, more persistent than the others, continued to interfere with his uvula and the posterior membrane of his tongue, ignoring all advice to desist, until after two or three weeks his people had to be called to take him away. These were lucky to be saved from the pitfalls of *siddhis*. Many others had their *siddhis* turned on them like boomerangs adversely affecting their physical and mental constitutions. *Siddhis* come naturally to the very few, due to yogic practices carried out during their previous *sadhana* and *karmic* determinations. These people are safe and sometimes helpful to humanity, if they behave reasonably in the *sadhana* of this life. They are likely to attain *mukti* if they are lucky and favourably disposed – *sattvic*, in other words.

'That which is always attained' refers to the Self, which is always present as the true nature of the ego whether the ego is conscious of it or not (see comment on verse thirty) before the birth of the body, during its existence and after its disintegration at death.

36. The thought 'I am not the body' helps one to meditate 'I am not this: I am THAT' and to abide as THAT. But why should one forever think 'I am THAT'? Does a man need always to think 'I am a man'? We are always THAT.

Verse thirty-two discourages the use of the thought 'I am not this'. However, this verse avers that even this negative meditation is useful to the extent that it leads to the positive meditation 'I am THAT'. But even the latter meditation appears to the *jnāni* superfluous, in that it is already granted that one is always THAT – 'That which is always attained' (verse thirty-five). That we are not the body any thinking man can discover for himself even without attempts at Self-realisation. For what dullard can find no difference between himself and, say, a chair or a table which does not move, think or speak like him, yet is made of the same elements? There must certainly be something in the human body, over and above what there is in the other objects. That something is life, or mind, or knowledge, or THAT, which *sadhakas* try to isolate from the body and perceive by itself, in its aloneness (*kaivalya*). That is the Self-realisation or self-cognition we are after.

37. The theory that in practical life duality prevails, whereas non-duality prevails in the (spiritual) attainment, is false. Whether one is still anxiously searching for the Self, or has actually attained it, one is not other than the tenth man.

Non-duality always prevails, whether viewed from the viewpoint of the world or from that of the realised yogi. The realisation of Self cannot turn the dual into non-dual. The truth of non-duality stands eternally true, as verse one has shown.

The *tenth man* refers to the story in which ten men travelled together. After fording a river, they decided to count themselves to make sure that none of them had been lost in the crossing. The man who counted his nine companions forgot to count himself, which resulted in their starting a search for the tenth man — actually always present as the counter himself. The same applies to man, who is always present as the eternal non-dual reality, but imagines himself always in duality due to his perception of multiplicity — 'I' and 'you', the chair, the door, the window and a million other objects. But the realised man is free from this false imagination: he knows himself to be the tenth man.

38. So long as a man feels himself the doer, he reaps the fruits of his actions. But as soon as he realises through enquiry who is the doer, the sense of doership drops off and the threefold karma comes to an end. This is the final Liberation.

Who is the doer? If the body is the doer then we have to attribute intelligence to it, an intelligence which it does not possess. The identification of the instrument of an act with the actor is the cause of much trouble. An illustration will be to the point. A man has a grudge against another man and plans to do away with him. He waylays him on a dark night, takes a stone and kills him with it. Who is the killer? Certainly not the stone, although it is the stone that has done the evil deed, nor is it the hand which holds the stone, nor the body of which the hand is a part, and which is as insentient, and therefore as innocent, as the stone. It is the mind which, with hatred, planned and executed the crime, using the instrumentality of the body and the stone. Therefore the mind is the empirical man, or ego who, so long as he believes himself to be the actor, has to reap the fruit of his actions effected through a body. But this belief, like the ego itself, is not permanent: it passes away immediately an enquiry is made into the identity of the doer.

The triple *karma* which hangs around the neck of the doer is made up of the *sanchita* (accumulated *karma*), the *prarabdha* (the *karma* which is destined to be worked out in this birth), and the *āgāmi* (the *karma* which becomes active in future births). The last class of *karma* will remain unfulfilled in the case of the person who has attained Liberation in the present body, and who will have no other births for *karma* to be worked in.

Questions are sometimes asked concerning the *jnāni's prarabdha* as to why it does not cease with his attainment of *jnāna*, thus sparing him suffering that may arise in the form of virulent disease, with which some famous *jnānis* are known to have been burdened. The answer is that the *prarabdha* of the *jnāni* had been allotted to him at or before birth, when he was still liable to the working of *karma* prior to his attainment of *jnāna*. As for his suffering, it is not as painful to him as it appears to others: it is greatly mitigated by the bliss of Realisation which unceasingly wells up in his heart.

Some Biblically-orientated Westerners seem to think that the suffering of the *jnāni* is due to his taking upon himself the sins of his disciples. *Vēdānta* denies the transference of sins and its responsibilities. Strict justice is the law of *karma* which tolerates no one to suffer for another's crimes, least of all a Guru, who comes to show the way to Truth. Far from being punished he is rewarded by the service, love, and devotion of the disciples. Thus the belief in a Salvation through the vicarious suffering of the Master is totally unacceptable in this path, where each man is regarded as working out his own liberation through hard work, self-purification, worship of the Guru, self-control, spiritual practices and a full sense of moral responsibility. In the whole

Vedantic literature one does not find a single reference to transference of sins, but always to *karma*.

39. Bondage and Liberation exist so long as thoughts of bondage and liberation exist. These come to an end when an enquiry is made into the nature of he who is bound or free, and the ever-present and ever-free Self is realised.

This has a close resemblance to the last verse, which makes the sense of doership to be the cause of karma. Likewise the sense of being bound or free makes bondage and liberation exist. Thus wrong notions about oneself are responsible for all the acts of destiny: birth, death, bondage, ignorance etc. But wrong notions can be rectified by right knowledge, which can be had only through an enquiry into the nature of the person who is the victim of the wrong notions. Then his real Self will reveal itself and will dispel all notions, all senses, and all thoughts, including the sense and thought of *jīva*hood (individuality) itself.

40. It is said that Liberation is with form or without form, or with and without form. Let me tell you that Liberation destroys all the three as well as the ego which distinguishes between them.

All these forms of liberation, some of which are said to take place in a disembodied state in some supersensuous worlds - *Vaikuntha*, *Satyaloka*, etc. are hypothetical. At best they offer encouragement to the *sadhakas* who are partial to them. The fact of the matter is that true and absolute Liberation results only from *jnāna* (knowledge of the Absolute), which alone can destroy ignorance, either in this body or in one of the following bodies. For there are no planes nor states of consciousness where radical salvation is possible, other than the waking state, i.e. in a body, where bondage and ignorance are felt and attempts for redemption made; least of all in the state of after-death where there is no body to feel the limitations and retributions of karma.

Therefore he who aspires to reach the highest has to exert himself hard here and now, preferably by the *vichāra* method which Bhagavan has so graciously propounded and so often reiterated in these verses. The determined *sadhaka* will not fail to verify these truths by his own experience if he puts them to the test, full of confidence in his own self and the unfailing silent support of the Master, who is not other than the very Reality he is so earnestly seeking, and who ever and ever abides in his own heart as Existence, Consciousness and Bliss – *Sat Chit Ananda*.

OM SHANTI SHANTI SHANTIHI

NOTES

Introduction

1 Talks with Ramana Maharshi, Ramanasramam, Tiruvannamalai, 3 vols.

Vivēkachūdāmani

1 In Sanskrit this is a play of words, as *vishaya* means sense objects and *visha* poison.
2 A name taken simply as an illustration.
3 This passage in brackets is inserted by the editor.
4 This refers to trial by ordeal, placing a hot iron in the hand of a suspected thief, who is burnt if guilty but not if innocent.
5 This does not imply that the disciple is in a state of ignorance, unable to differentiate between reality and illusion, but, on the contrary, that he is now established in the Non-duality beyond all opposites, even the opposite of being and non-being.
6 Even *Ishvara*, the personal God, is a condensation or manifestation of absolute Being and therefore to some extent a limitation. Even this is transcended in the state without impurities, without any ego-sense.
7 Taken here simply as a specimen name.
8 i adhyatmika, ii adhibhoutika, iii adhidaivika

Dakshināmūrti

1 *Chinmudra*: literally, the gesture of pure Consciousness, is indicated by making the thumb and the index finger touch each other and spreading out the remaining fingers. This gesture not only symbolises unity behind multiplicity but also the identity of the individual self and the supreme Self.
2 There are many traditional *mudras* or postures of the hands which are used in Indian dancing and iconography, each of which has its own meaning.

3   The supreme Guru is the spiritual north pole and therefore
    traditionally faces southwards.

Ātma Bōdha

1   The allusion is to the story of a lady wearing a precious
    necklace, who suddenly forgot where it was, grew anxious,
    looked for it everywhere and even asked others to help, until
    a kind friend pointed out that it was round the seeker's own
    neck.

Vichāra Mani Mālā

1   *Upāsana* is the uninterrupted meditation upon a deity or a
    form or a word like Om until one becomes that deity or
    form or word. It is a technique which is not generally
    followed nowadays. Its modern equivalent is *bhakti*
    (devotion).

2   *Vedantic* sayings are of two kinds, namely chief and secondary.
    The texts which propound the nature of the *jīva* and *Brahman*
    are secondary texts. They produce indirect (intellectual)
    knowledge. The chief texts propound the identity of the *jīva*
    and *Brahman*. They produce direct knowledge.

3   The four qualifications are (1) discrimination between what
    is eternal and what is fleeting (*nityāntiya vastu vivēka*) (2)
    absence of desire for the enjoyment of the fruits of (one's
    actions) in this world and the next (*ihāmutrartha phala bhoga
    virāga*) (3) the possession of the six virtues which are
    control of the mind (*sama*), control of the sense-organs
    (*dama*), cessation of activity (*uparati*), fortitude (*titiksha*),
    faith in the scriptures and the guru (*sraddha*) and
    concentration of mind (*samādhāna*); and (4) yearning for
    liberation.

4   The three steps are hearing (*sravana*), reflection (*manana*)
    and uninterrupted contemplation (*nididhyāsana*).

GLOSSARY

A

advaita: non-duality, often incorrectly termed 'monism'

āgāmi karma: actions good and bad, expected to bear fruit in future births

aham: I; embodied self; soul

aham sphurana: the throb of Self-bliss in the heart

aham svarūpa: one's true nature

ahamkāra (or ahankāra): the ego-self

ajnāna: ignorance; knowledge of diversity

ananda: bliss

anartha: evil, worthless

antahkarana: instruments of inner perception

antarmukha drishti: inward vision

apāna: one of the ten vital airs

aprāna: beyond manifest life; devoid of life

āsana: yogic posture

astānga-yōga: yoga consisting of eight stages of discipline

ātman (or ātma):   self; principle of life and sensation

ātma dhyāna   contemplation on the Self

ātmanusandhāna   contemplation on the Self

ātma vichāra: enquiry into the Self

avidyā: nescience, ignorance

B

Bhagavān: a commonly used name for God; a title used for one like Sri Ramana who is recognised as having realized his identity with the Self

bahirmukha drishti: outward turned consciousness

bhakta: a devotee

bhakti: devotion and love

Bhārata: a form of address used by Sri Krishna towards Arjuna in the Bhagavad Gita, meaning a shining soul

bhāvana: continued meditation; steady concentration of mind

gunās: the three fundamental qualities, tendencies, or
                        stresses which underlie all manifestation;
                        sattva, rajas, and *tamas,* characterized as white,
                        red and black respectively

H

hōma: sacrifice in fire
hridayam: the Heart (*hridi* + *ayam* = centre + this); the
                        seat of Consciousness at the right side of the
                        chest, as experienced and expounded by Sri
                        Ramana Maharshi

I

Indra: the Lord of the *devas*; the first student of
                        Brahma viydā; the Divine Mother was his
                        teacher
Isa: the supreme Lord
Ishvara: the name of the supreme Lord indicating his
                        lordship of the worlds

J

jaganmāyā: the mystery of the world
jīva: the individual soul or ego
jīvan mukta: one who has realized the supreme identity
                        while still in the body
jīvan mukti: deliverance while yet in this life
jnāna: knowledge of the Absolute transcending form
                        and formlessness
jnāna mārga: the path of knowledge
jnāni: a Self-realized person, a sage; one who has
                        attained realization by the path of knowledge

K

Kailās: a mountain in the Himalayas reputed to be the
                        abode of Lord Siva
kaivalya: absolute Oneness; final emancipation; one of
                        the 108 Upanishads

Brahma:	Lord of Creation; God as the Creator
Brahman:	the Absolute
buddhi:	intellect; one of the four aspects of the internal organ

C

chakra:	a wheel, a yogic centre of concentration
chandrāyana:	expiatory fast for a full month, commencing from the full moon, food being diminished every day by one handful during the dark fortnight, and increased in like manner during the bright fortnight
chit:	absolute intelligence or consciousness
chitta:	the mental mode turned towards objects; that aspect of the mind in which impressions are stored

D

dahara vidyā:	contemplation of the deity in the cavity of the heart
dēva:	a god or celestial being
dēvata:	a deity
Dēvi:	the divine Mother or a goddess
dharma:	virtuous deeds; harmonious life; a person's natural duty; inherent qualities
dhyāna:	contemplation; the seventh rung in the ladder of eight-fold yoga
drik:	subject
drisya:	object

G

Ganapati:	the elder son of Lord Siva, the remover of obstacles; the same as Lord Ganesha, the chief of Lord Siva's hosts
Gudākēsa:	an epithet of Arjuna for having conquered sleep; Lord Krishna uses this term in addressing Arjuna

kali yuga:	the last of four ages of the world, namely *Krita, Trēta, Dwāpara,* and *Kali; Kali* is reckoned as having begun in 3102 B.C.
kāma:	desire; physical love
karma:	action, work, deeds; also fruits of action accumulating in three ways as *sanchita, prārabdha,* and *āgāmi;* destiny
karma mārga:	the path of ritual, religious duties, and action
kēvala kumbhaka:	retention of breath leading to stilling of the mind, without inhalation or exhalation
kshētra:	a sacred place of pilgrimage; in yoga, city, or the field of body
kshētrajna:	the conscious principle (known) in the field of the body; the absolute witness aware of the three states of the self; waking, dream, and sleep
kundalinī:	the mystic circle of three-and-a-half coils situated in the umbilical region; the yogic principle of serpent power; primal *māyā*

L

laya:	absorption; in yoga, absorption of breath and mind in the heart
lingam:	a vertical column of stone with a rounded end, symbol of the unmanifest Siva

M

maharshi (maha rishi):	great rishi or sage
mahat:	the intellectual principle as source of *ahamkāra* — from the Absolute emanates the unmanifest, from it *mahat* and from *mahat* the *ahamkāra*
mahātma:	a lofty soul; highly spiritual person; master in tune with the infinite
mahāvākya:	the four main sentences, proclaiming the truth of *Brahman,* one each from the Itareya (Aitareya) Upanishad of Rig Veda, Brihadaranyaka of Yajur Veda, Chandogya of Sama Veda and Mandukya of Atharva Veda;

	one of the 108 Upanishads explaining the *mahāvakyas*
Mahēswara:	one of the five aspects of Lord Siva, as veiling the truth from souls, till their *karma* is completely worked out
manana:	contemplation; the second of the three stages of *Vēdāntic* realization
manas:	mind, reason, mentality; also used for the aggregate of *chitta, buddhi, manas,* and *ahamkāra*
mantram (*mantra*):	cosmic sound forms of the Vedas, used for worship and prayer; seed letters for meditation on the form of the Lord; ritualistic incantation
marana:	the art of causing death through supernatural powers
math:	a meeting place and abode of sadhus
māyā:	illusion, false appearance; manifestation or illusion personified
mithyā:	the false
mōksha:	liberation; final emancipation; release from transmigration
mouna:	silence; the inexpressible; truth of *Brahman,* expressed by the *Brahman*-knower by his mere abidance in stillness
mudra:	hand-pose in worship and dance
mukta:	a liberated person
mukti:	liberation
mutt:	see *math*

N

nādi:	the 72,000 nerves of the body conveying the life force, of which *idā, pingalā* and *sushumnā* are the three main ones; in the state of *samādhi* all of them are merged in the single *para* or *amrita nādi*
nāsha:	destruction
nididhyāsana:	the last of the three stages of *Vēdāntic* realization; uninterrupted contemplation

nirāsa:	desirelessness
nirvikalpa samādhi:	the highest state of concentration, in which the soul loses all sense of being different from the universal Self, but a temporary state from which there is return to ego-consciousness
nischala bhāva:	immobility; steadfastness; eternity
nishthā:	abidance in firm meditation
niyama:	discipline: religious duties as ordained for the second of the eight stages of yoga

P

padma:	lotus; a yoga posture in which the right foot is placed on the left thigh and the left foot on the right thigh
paramapada:	the supreme state
paramārthika:	an epithet of Arjuna, meaning he who destroys his enemy
Paramātman:	the true Self
Pārtha:	Arjuna, the son of Pritha, another name for Kunti, his mother
prajnāna ghana:	*Brahman*; the Absolute, immutable knowledge
prakriti:	primordial substance out of which all things are created; the primal nature
pramada:	swerving from abidance in the Absolute
prāna:	the first of the ten vital airs centred in the heart
pranava japa:	incantation of Om
prānāyāma:	breath control
prārabdha karma:	that part of destiny due to past action (*karma*) which bears fruit in the present birth
Prasthāna Traya:	the triple canon of *Vēdānta*; the three *Vēdāntic* scriptural authorities: Upanishads, Brahma Sutras, *Bhagavad Gita*
pratyāhāra:	withdrawal of the senses from objectivity: the fifth rung in the ladder of yoga
Purānas:	eighteen sacred books ascribed to Vyasa, dealing with primary and secondary creation, genealogy of kings, etc

purānam:	fullness, infinite
purusha:	spirit, soul, the living principle
purushārtha:	human ends, objectives worthy of human pursuit, *dharma, artha, kāma* and *mōksha*

R

Rāghava:	an epithet of Sri Rama as belonging to the line of Raghu
rāja yōga:	the principle system of yoga as taught by Patanjali
rajas:	one of the three primal qualities, described as red, the principle of activity (see *guna*)
rishi:	sage (see also *maharshi*)
Rudra:	Lord Siva in one of his five aspects; God as destroyer

S

Sadā Siva:	the supreme Lord as eternal goodness
sadguru:	the great Master, the true or perfect Guru
sādhana:	a path towards liberation
sādhu:	an ascetic or one who has renounced the world in quest of liberation
sahasradala:	the thousand-petalled lotus; the centre of illumination experienced in the crown of the head on the yogic path
sākshin:	witness
samāna:	one of the ten vital airs
sanchita karma:	accumulated *karma* of former births that still remains to be experienced
sankalpa:	volition, mental activity, thought, tendencies, and attachment
sānkhya:	one of the systems of Indian philosophy
sannyāsa:	renunciation
sannyāsin:	one who has renounced the world
sāntōdānta:	one who is calm and self-controlled
sarvātma bhāva:	the state of experiencing the Self as all; abidance in the oneness of Being
sāstras:	scriptures

sat:	existence; pure Being
satchidānanda:	Being-Consciousness-Bliss
sattva:	tendency to purity; one of the three *gunas*
savikalpa samādhi:	a state of consciousness in which the distinction between the knower, knowledge and known is not yet lost
Shakti (or *Sakti*):	the manifesting energy of a divine aspect, represented mythologically as the wife of a God
siddha:	one endowed with supernatural powers and capable of performing miracles: one who has accomplished the end
siddhi:	realization, attainment; also supernatural powers
Siva:	the supreme Lord; one of the Hindu Trinity
Sivōham:	the incantation: 'I am Siva'
Skanda:	the younger son of Lord Siva; the leader of the divine hosts; the same as Lord Subrahmanya
Smriti:	authoritative Hindu scriptures other than the Vēdas (*Sruti*)
sraddha:	earnestness, faith, a faithful acquisition of theoretical knowledge of Truth
sravana:	hearing of the truth, from the Master
Sruti:	Vēdas, heard by the sages in their transcendental state and transmitted to disciples by word of mouth
sushupti:	deep sleep
svarūpa nishtā:	abidance in the Self

T

tamas:	darkness, ignorance; one of the three *gunas*
tanmaya nishtā:	abidance in the Self
tapas:	religious austerities
tat:	That; *Brahman*
tattva jnāna:	knowledge of *Brahman* or *ātman*
tat-tvam-asi:	'That thou Art'
turiya:	the fourth state; the witness Consciousness —

ever present and unchanging as against the changing states of waking, dreaming, and deep sleep

U

udāna: one of the ten vital airs, whose seat is in the neck

upadēsa: the spiritual guidance or teaching given by a Guru

Upanishads: philosophical writings forming part of the Vedas

V

Vaikunta: the heaven of Vishnu

vairāgya: freedom from worldly desires; dispassion

vāsanās: predispositions, tendencies, or propensities of the mind in the present life due to the experiences of former lives

Vāsudēva: Lord Krishna, as the son of Vasudēva, the Lord whose manifestation all this world is; one of the 108 Upanishads showing the path of Vāsudēva

Vēda: the sacred books of the Hindus: Rig, Yajur, Sama, and Atharva, revealed through the rishis

vēdānta: the absolute Truth as established by the Upanishads, Brahma Sutras, and Bhagavad Gita as interpreted by Sri Vyāsa; the end or consummation of the Vēdas

veena: a string instrument

vichāra: enquiry into the truth of the Self

vidēhamukta: a liberated being after he has left the body

vidēhamukti: Self-realization after leaving the body

vijnāna: knowledge; discriminating the real from the unreal

vijnānamārga: the path of discriminate knowledge

Vishnu: God as preserver; one of the Hindu Trinity

vishaya vāsanās: predisposition towards sense enjoyments

vivēka: discrimination

viyōga:	separation
vyāna:	one of the ten vital airs, causing the circulation of blood and pervading all the body
vyavahārika:	the phenomenal or empirical

Y

yama:	self-control, the first rung in the ladder of the eight-fold yoga; abstention from lying, killing, theft, lust, covetousness